you know you're in
michigan when...

Some Other Books in the Series

You Know You're In Series

you know you're in
michigan when...

101 Quintessential Places, People, Events, Customs, Lingo, and Eats of the Great Lakes State

Colleen Burcar

INSIDERS' GUIDE®

GUILFORD, CONNECTICUT
AN IMPRINT OF THE GLOBE PEQUOT PRESS

INSIDERS' GUIDE®

Copyright © 2005 by The Globe Pequot Press

Text design and illustrations by Linda R. Loiewski

Library of Congress Cataloging-in-Publication Data
Burcar, Colleen.
 You know you're in Michigan when— : 101 quintessential places, people, events, customs, lingo, and eats of the Great Lakes state / Colleen Burcar.— 1st ed.
      p. cm. — (You know you're in series)
 Includes index.
 ISBN 0-7627-3812-X
 1. Michigan—Guidebooks. 2. Michigan—Miscellanea. 3. Michigan—Description and travel—Miscellanea. I. Title. II. Series.
 F564.3.B87 2005
 977.4—dc22

                                                        2005010934

Manufactured in the United States of America
First Edition/First Printing

To my wonderful husband, Bryan Becker, who is living proof that "You Know You're in Michigan When You Find Your Soul Mate and Love of Your Life"

about the author

Colleen Burcar has been a radio and television reporter, and a columnist for the *Detroit News*. In addition to her work as a freelance magazine writer, speaker, media consultant, and author of *Michigan Curiosities,* her voice can be heard on a host of commercials. Her roots are 100 percent Michigan—her father was born in the Upper Peninsula, and Burcar remains a U.P. "aristocratic" name today—and she's lived in the state her entire life. She resides in Bloomfield Hills with her husband, Bryan Becker, and their toy poodle, Chloe.

to the reader

Every proud American regards their home state as unique, but those of us from Michigan stand alone as those who can honestly boast that their state is one-of-a-kind. Aside from island communities, we are singularly distinguished as the only two-part state in the country. Divided by water, bridged by concrete, we stand together with heart.

Our pulse can be felt from our farms, forests, and festivals, to our manufacturing, music, and mosquitoes. We are a four-season natural beauty, with a flawless complexion that radiates the shades of the summer sun or the harvest moon. Plop on a pair of our home-grown Hush Puppies, and our feet are as comfortable walking through April showers as they are trekking to the cottage through four feet of snow.

Whether you're a new resident, a first-time visitor, or full-blooded Michiganian, I hope this compilation will show you how, no matter what the weatherperson says, we live life to the fullest 365 days a year. May the following pages help you assimilate the true taste and feel of our core, as it records at 101 beats per minute.

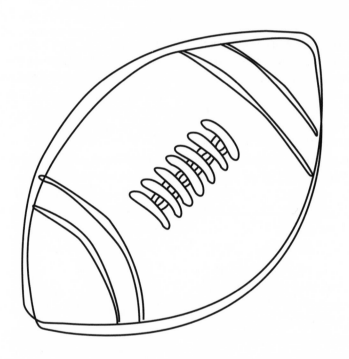

you know you're in
michigan when...
...all-you-can-eat is chicken

Which day of the week do chickens hate most? Fry Day.

In Frankenmuth, every day is Fry Day. During the town's formative years, Theodore Fischer looked out at his chicken coop and perhaps thought to himself, "If we fry them, they will come."

Today, the famous all-you-can-eat chicken dinners have become synonymous with the town that now ranks as one of Michigan's top tourist attractions, drawing more than three million visitors each year.

How long do chickens work? Around the cluck.

Two of Mr. Fischer's landmark restaurants, now both owned by members of the Zehnder family, have been filling hungry stomachs since the early 1900s with a poultry bill to rival the federal deficit. During the course of a year, Zehnder's, America's largest family-owned restaurant, fries up 840,000 pounds of chicken to serve in its ten dining rooms with seating for 1,500, while right across the street the 1,200-seat Bavarian Inn Restaurant sizzles another 750,000 pounds. They say Mother's Day and weekends in October are their busiest. A typical week serves only 20,000.

What do chickens serve at birthday parties? Coop cakes.

More than 10,000 birthday cakes annually fly off the shelves of Zehnder's Bakery, though the celebrated stollen fruit bread (which also accompanies the all-you-can-eat platters) is their top-selling baked good.

After biting off more than you can chew, you can relax and be chauffeured by horse and carriage through quaint Bavarian-inspired streets to peer through antiques shop windows.

Both restaurants are on South Main Street. For more information, call Zehnder's at (800) 863–7999 or visit www.zehnders.com. You can talk to the folks at the Bavarian Inn at (800) 228–2742 or go to www.bavarianinn .com for online reservations at least forty-eight hours in advance.

Finally, where do all these silly chicken jokes come from? A yoke book, naturally.

All-You-Can-Eat Chicken Dinners:

Culinary feasts served by two of the largest restaurants in America, both in Frankenmuth.

Henry Wadsworth Longfellow may have been from Maine, but he found the perfect setting for his epic poem "Song of Hiawatha" in Michigan's Tahquamenon Falls. Situated in the Upper Peninsula, these majestic waterfalls are the second largest east of the Mississippi, placing behind Niagara Falls. They rush, gush, and thrust up to 50,000 gallons of water per second during the spring melt, compared to Niagara's 150,000 gallons.

In reality, Tahquamenon Falls (pronounced TUH-kwam-a-NEN) is a pair of fraternal twins, unimaginatively named Upper and Lower. The Upper Falls is the better-looking, big brother, standing nearly 50 feet tall and 200 feet wide, overshadowing the Lower, a cascading series of smaller falls.

First time visitors are in awe of the water's rich bronze tan, which doesn't come from iron, minerals, rust, mud, or a bottle. The healthy amber glow is a result of tannins leached by the cedar, hemlock, and spruce in the swamps produced by the river's drainage.

Another Tahquamenon trademark is the fluffy foam creating artistic patterns both above and below the falls. Nothing artificial here either. The softness of the water combined with the unique churning motion claims responsibility for the fanciful froth.

One of the easiest ways to explore the 40,000-acre Tahquamenon Falls State Park is through the eyes of the Toonerville Trolley, the longest 24-inch gauge railroad in the country. Family owned and operated for some eighty years, the train is reminiscent of its namesake, the rickety and unpredictable Toonerville cartoon trolley popular in the early 1900s.

For more information on the hiking, boating, and camping facilities within Tahquamenon Falls State Park on Highway 123 in Paradise, call (906) 492–3415. The Toonerville Trolley chugs along mid-June through early October. Call (888) 77–TRAIN.

Amber Falls:

Massive, muscular waterfalls, tanned to perfection, displaying brute force through their mighty roar.

you know you're in
michigan when...
... an apple a day means the orchards will stay

Lest there be any question, apples are the core of Michigan's fruit business, peeling—er, make that *reeling*—in $150 million to the state's economy annually. At last count, there were 1,000 apple growers who kept Johnny Appleseed busy planting more than eight million apple trees on nearly 42,500 acres.

Michigan is the third-largest apple producer in the nation, yielding twenty million bushels a year. The tried-and-true Red Delicious remains the favorite variety, followed by Golden Delicious and the rising star, Gala.

What happens to all that fiber-filled fruit? Naturally it gets eaten but not always naturally. The popularity and convenience of processed food has extended to the apple industry, affecting 75 percent of Michigan's crop. Today when someone says he's hitting the sauce he could mean he's diving into a bowl of applesauce or a glass of fermented apple cider.

It wouldn't be autumn without a trip to one of the sixty-three cider mills in the state where apples are turned into an unpasteurized drink, usually consumed with a tasty fried doughnut.

With the increasing awareness of healthy eating, McDonald's now offers an option of

Apples:

Michigan is home to many cider mills, in addition to providing McDonald's with all the apples in their Happy Meals.

sliced apples with each Happy Meal, making Michigan farmers even happier. That's because 100 percent of all Happy Meal apples were born and bred in Michigan.

Think twice the next time you reach for a cup of coffee. The Michigan Apple Commission says apples are far more efficient than caffeine in keeping people awake in the morning. The sugar in the apples, combined with the chewing action, creates an increased state of alertness.

Finally, one note of caution: Do not store your apples near your potatoes. Ripened apples emit ethylene gas, giving the potatoes a bad case of premature sprouting.

...you can watch the nuts and bolts of your vehicle's assembly

Automaker extraordinaire Henry Ford was dishing up inspirational quotes for the soul long before chicken soup made it out of the kitchen. Born, bred, and buried in Michigan, his lips gave breath to classics like "Whether you think you can or think you can't, you're right"; "My best friend is the one who brings out the best in me"; and "Don't find fault. Find a remedy."

That last phrase triggered the solution for Ford's objective to "build a car for the great multitude" by creating a conveyor-belt assembly line that would lower the price of a Model T from $850 to $280. By 1914 his revolutionary manufacturing techniques took an earlier production time of 728 minutes per completed chassis to just 93 minutes.

To combat high employee turnover, Ford instituted a new $5.00-a-day wage policy. Even with the huge pay raise, the National Organization for Women and ACLU would have had a field day with the policy, which excluded married women and scrutinized the men to make sure they were avoiding "social ills" like drinking and gambling.

Dearborn's 2,000-acre Rouge Plant, once the largest anywhere, opened in 1924 for public tours, drawing 250,000 annually to wow over the ninety-three structures and 120 miles of conveyors.

Suspended in 1980 for plant renovations, the visits have begun again. Only now the look is high-polished. The five-part tours are razzle-dazzle, Disney-infused multimedia spectaculars, accompanied by an eight-screen theater-in-the-round and a stroll on the catwalk to eye the new F-150 pickups, come to life on the assembly line. Advance ticket reservations are highly recommended. They can be purchased online at www.thehenryford.org or by calling (313) 982–6001.

Auto Assembly Line:

Ford's Rouge Plant is the one place production-line assembly receives an audience's standing ovation.

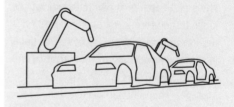

you know you're in
michigan when...
...the cars are the stars

Only in Michigan could you get 17,500 people to shell out $400 apiece to stand around in black tie for three hours staring at cars while sipping cheap champagne from plastic flutes. There's not a morsel of food in sight during Preview Night for the North American International Auto Show (NAIAS), generally the coldest, snowiest January night of the year. It's also a particularly tough night on feet since evening gowns don't have as much appeal when paired with Uggs.

But the crowds do come to see and be seen next to the latest vehicles while raising millions of dollars for eleven children's charities, although likely not more than a dozen people could name even one of those charities.

The private opening night has been a fashionable scene since 1976, decades after the formerly titled Detroit Auto Show began in a beer garden in 1907. From thirty-three vehicles then to more than 700 now, Michigan's auto industry knows how to put its best wheel forward. Since going international in 1989, 853 vehicles have had their "premiere"—or as they say in the auto industry, "reveal"—at Cobo Hall, which for ten days becomes the world's most exclusive parking garage.

The prestigious NAIAS continues to rank third in the country for the estimated income's economic impact, behind Atlanta's 1996 Summer Olympics and the Daytona 500.

Visitors come from sixty countries and forty-two states (no one identifies the eight holdouts) to be in the company of the stars, whether they're former presidents (Eisenhower and Clinton among them) or celebs like Celine Dion. And, oh yes, the cars.

For more information on dates and prices for the next vehicular extravaganza, visit www.naias.com.

Auto Show:

Ten days of stellar car-watching, from today's latest to the concepts of tomorrow.

you know you're in
michigan when...
...you share breakfast with 60,786

Two words will get almost anyone out of bed early: *free food*. Each year, on the second Saturday in June, more than 60,000 people chow down at the World's Longest Breakfast Table—all 2,700 feet of it—spread out over five blocks in Battle Creek. The cereal capital made it into the Guinness Book with this event, an annual tradition since 1956.

Corn flakes were invented, albeit accidentally, in Battle Creek. While cooking wheat in their Seventh-Day Adventist Health Spa, the Kellogg brothers were called out unexpectedly. Upon their return they found a batch of dried, stale, flakey grains. A few minutes in the oven and the taste improved, and in 1894 the cereal industry was born.

During the early 1900s there were more than eighty cereal companies, but one by one they went the way of Smurfberry Crunch. Burnt food we'll eat; blue food is another story.

Cereal City, USA, is now a major infotainment attraction where you can view a simulated cereal production line complete with eau de cornflake spraying through the air, hug Tony the Tiger, or become a "famous flake" with your own face projected on a

Battle Creek:

The cereal capital sets a breakfast table fit for a king, his court, and twelve small countries.

cereal box. They also offer Froot Loop sundaes for purchase seven days a week. (Call 269–962–6230.)

If you're wondering about the city's name, yes, combat of sorts did occur locally between Potawatomi Indians and a surveyor alongside an obscure trickle of water. Possibly the most excitement of its time, it's why the municipality of Milton became forever known as Battle Creek.

For information regarding the freebie breakfast to share with 60,786 of your best friends, call the Greater Battle Creek Visitor and Convention Bureau at (800) 397–2240.

you know you're in
michigan when...
...the winters can be "un-bearable"

Anyone who's spent time in Michigan will remember the renowned "bear dumps," of the Upper Peninsula (U.P.), more familiar to non-Yoopers as small-town landfills. In lieu of a drive-in movie, a typical night's entertainment would be to head to the dump at dusk armed with marshmallows and wait in your car for the bear procession to begin.

'Long about 1990, modern-day waste management changed all that, closing the last of the trashy theaters and ending the G-rated bear viewings.

Illogically, the state says bear-feeding isn't illegal, sanctioning restaurants in towns like Silver City and White Pine to put out food in hopes of attracting both bears and customers.

At last count, the state had some 12,000 black bears, with the highest concentration in the U.P. However, with each passing year, in true Michigan fashion, more and more are growing tired of the long winters and heading south. The Department of Natural Resources says most often it's young males seeking independence and a new crop of women who find refuge in the big cities of Muskegon and Lansing.

Oswald's Bear Ranch, the largest exclusively-bear ranch in the U.S., is the one place where you can still visit the furry big guys in their somewhat-natural environment. Newberry's Dean Oswald is the Pied Piper to dozens of bears, housing and feeding them in 10- to 15-acre fenced habitats until they go into hibernation. Then he, like the wayward baby bear, heads south.

Open to walk around every day from Memorial Day weekend through Labor Day, Oswald's can be found by heading 4 miles north of Newberry on Highway 123 to Deer Park Road. Turn left and travel another 4 miles until you see bear signs to guide you the rest of the way. Call (906) 293–3147 or visit www.oswaldsbearranch.com.

Bears:

A trip down south is helping them survive their displacement from the U.P. dumps they used to call home.

you know you're in
michigan when...
...The Big House means football

Ask almost anyone in Ann Arbor where they're going on a football Saturday and they'll promptly respond "The Big House," the name affectionately given to the University of Michigan stadium by ABC sports commentator Keith Jackson.

The biggest college stadium in the country started athletic director Fielding Yost's vision. Constructed in 1927 for $950,000 on land housing an underground spring, the high water table meant that nearly 75 percent of the seventy-two-row stadium had to be built below ground level.

Allowing 18 inches a seat for each ticket holder, opening-day capacity was 84,401. But renovations over the years have expanded that number to today's seating for 107,501. The largest crowd ever in attendance was recorded on November 22, 2003, when 112,118 watched U of M beat Ohio State, 35–21. The extra 5,000 came from those in the band and press box, as well as ushers and utility workers. What isn't known is the location of former coach and athletic director Fritz Crisler's seat. It remains a mystery but accounts for the added "one" stated in the capacity number.

In 1998 a bright-yellow $500,000 parapet dubbed the "halo" was added, emblazoned with a winged helmet and words from the school's theme song, "The Victors." A blaze of fury came from the ultra-traditional alumni, who criticized its color, the size of the letters and symbols, and its gaudiness. In January 2000 the university's president, Lee Bollinger, acquiesced, and another $100,000 was spent to tear down the new addition.

When you enter The Big House, you may be searched. There's a long list of prohibited items, including noisemakers and marsh-mallows, the latter a weapon of choice wielded by students against camera crews.

Ticket prices seem to increase every year, yet that hasn't stopped the faithful from fill-ing the stands at more than 170 consecu-tive home games with more than 100,000 people, giving the University of Michigan the home-attendance title of the nation. For your chance at a ticket, contact (866) 296–MTIX or www.mgoblue.com.

The Big House:

Fans say the seats in this stadium have been getting smaller. Officials say they've always allowed 18 inches per ticket. You be the judge.

Mention *Big Three* in Michigan and two things immediately come to mind: cars and pizza.

Perhaps by the skin of its teeth, Detroit (a.k.a. the Motor City) remains the Auto Capital of the World. At one time, 85 percent of America's vehicles were made in Michigan, but rising labor costs and tough foreign competition have caused a Titanic shift.

The Big Three auto makers were real people. Model T creator Henry Ford promoted individuality with "You can have any color you want as long as it's black" (black dries quicker); General Motors founder, one-time millionaire, and compulsive shopper William Durant died penniless in New York in 1946; and Walter Chrysler was a former railroad worker and president of General Motors' Buick division before starting his namesake auto firm at age fifty.

The state's other bulky trio makes their dough out of spicier ingredients. Michigan is home to headquarters for Domino's, America's number-two pizza seller; Little Caesar's, number four; and Hungry Howie's, lucky number thirteen. Together they represent 11,528 outlets globally, just shy of number-one Pizza Hut's 12,053, placing Michigan on the cusp of becoming Pizza Capital of the World.

> ### Big Three:
> Auto makers and pizza makers are neck and neck in the saucy, hard-driving competition to rule their industries.

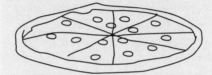

Flat buns and curvy fenders share a similar Italian heritage. The word *pizza* was first heard 3,000 years ago in Naples, a derivative of *picea,* a collection of multicolored ingredients thrown in a pan. *Automobile* combines the Greek word *auto* meaning *self* with Latin's mobils or *moving,* a word first spoken in the fourteenth century by Italian engineer Francesco di Giorgio Martini as he drew up plans for a human-powered carriage with four wheels. Who knew then that an auto and a good martini should never be mixed?

Michigan is full of beans. Okay, it's a trite, overused statement, but can you think of a better way to describe a state that is the number-one black bean producer in America, as well as being first in the production of small red beans and cranberry beans? With an output of 400 million pounds of beans a year, that amounts to, well, let's just say it's more than a hill of beans.

The bean capital of Michigan is in the state's thumb, which began tilling the land in the 1880s. World War II saw an increased demand by servicemen and -women everywhere. Today the health benefits of this highest source of protein outside of meat—with its cholesterol-reducing qualities and low sodium and fat content—have taken beans out of the category of a "poor man's meal" into a position of global importance.

Growers export roughly every other row of dry beans they raise, with 90 percent of the total crop finding a new home in Italy, Portugal, and Spain. Our black beans ship to Brazil and Mexico. Don't think these locales settle for just any beans. It's not unusual in major cities in Mexico to see listed on the menu, "Michigan Black Beans" or the more alluring translation, "Habas Negras de Michigan."

Black Beans:

Michigan is America's number-one producer of these glamorous legumes.

As for America, we're beginning to get on the bean bandwagon—or make that vehicle a Jaguar. In 2000 the Jaguar Black Bean became officially registered, the result of years of work by the Michigan State University and USDA breeding team. (And you thought only animals had registered breeders.)

Our country's leaders have their own love fest going on with our bean. Every day on the menu in the U.S. Senate restaurant, you'll find Michigan Bean Soup. Furthermore, July has been declared National Baked Beans Month, which may make for some powerful Independence Day fireworks.

you know you're in
michigan when...
... your wallet has more photos of your boat than of your family

With 11,000 inland lakes and 36,000 miles of rivers and streams, Michigan's secondary moniker, "Water Wonderland," is an obvious choice. (For a few years in the mid-1960s, though, license plates proclaimed us the "Winter Water Wonderland," a polite way of saying we're freezing our buns on the ice.)

After the first thaw, 1,000,337 registered boats are chomping at the bow to become the first on Corpse Pond or Mud Lake (the latter is the state's number-one water name), helping us retain our top ranking. In 2002 California initially declared itself the winner, until a 200,000-boat accounting error was discovered and dropped the surfing sailors to third place. Kayaks and canoes aren't figured into the million-plus; neither are boats less than 16 feet without motors.

The title "Recreational Motor Capital" conceivably belongs to Grosse Ile, a posh island south of Detroit. Not only does it claim to have more outboard motors per person than anywhere else in the country, it's also home to Cameron Waterman, who invented them.

Forget Mr. Ole Evinrude. Dated encyclopedias mistakenly credit him with the first outboard in 1909, but Waterman had his motor running in 1905. Three years later Waterman Marine Motor Company had already sold more than 6,000 outboards, a preamble to the more-than-eight-million in operation today.

You can view the inner workings of the first chain-driven outboard on display at Dossin Great Lakes Museum on Belle Isle. (Open Saturday and Sunday or by appointment; call 313–833–9721.)

Boating:

Michigan is the boating capital of America, with more registered boats than any other state.

you know you're in
michigan when...
...Christmas shopping is *really* big 361 days a year

'Tis the season to walk the length of 1.7 football fields, ogle 100,000 brilliantly colored lights, and be thankful you don't have to pay the $900-a-day electric bill. 'Tis an everyday occurrence at the world's largest Christmas store in Frankenmuth.

Bronner's is the Michigan store drawing two million guests a year, all determined to create the picture-perfect Christmas through the purchase of 1.3 million ornaments, 700,000 feet of garland, and more than 530 miles of light sets. The busiest day on record was the day after Thanksgiving, November 26, 1994, when 25,981 shoppers occupied the entire complex, including gardens—the equivalent of five and a half football fields, their favorite form of measurement.

Advertising isn't targeted at only state residents. More than sixty billboards line Interstate 75 almost from end to end, the farthest being near Ocala, Florida, to the north of Disney World.

This enchanting world is the brainchild of Wally Bronner and his wife, Irene, who started their lifelong holiday in 1945, expanding to a trio of buildings and eventually opening their current single free-standing structure on June 8, 1977, followed by much-needed expansions in 1991 and 2002. Their growth reminds one of a girdle with stretched-out elastic holding things in place until there's simply no room left.

Bronner's CHRISTmas Wonderland:

Need a shot of Christmas in July? Bronner's 56-foot Silent Night Chapel and its megastore give tranquility and hustle-bustle any time.

If there's anything your Christmas heart has ever desired, you're sure to find it here. Some 6,000 different styles of ornaments are perpetually on display, including ornaments that say *Merry Christmas* in more than seventy languages.

They're all yours for the buying, 361 days a year. Of course, you can always phone in your order, like John "The Duke" Wayne did on December 15, 1976, when he realized his Christmas wouldn't be complete without a Santa suit from Bronner's.

Bronner's CHRISTmas Wonderland sits at 25 Christmas Lane in Frankenmuth. Call (989) 652–9931 or (800) ALL–YEAR. You can order from their Web site at www.bronners.com.

you know you're in
michigan when...
... you're greeted by two 20-foot grizzlies

When Cabela's Sporting Goods opened its doors in 2000, the fight began. It quickly touted itself as Michigan's Number-One tourist attraction, and just as rapidly others disagreed. How could one store near the Ohio border in Dundee (population 2,056) claim that title?

The debate may never be settled without an arm-wrestling match between the two grizzly bears standing guard in the parking lot. (The 17,000-pound, 20-foot fighting bears, crafted by former Buffalo Bills lineman-turned-artist Mike Hamby, are, without contention, the world's largest bronze wildlife sculpture.)

This 225,000-square-foot store is perhaps the only retail establishment where people do appear more as tourists than customers, exiting their fully stocked SUVs armed with unloaded rifles (for repair) or loaded cameras ready to capture a shot of one of the hundreds of animals on display, here after a session with a taxidermist's skillful hands: mountain goats, elephants, water buffalo, and more. The fish, however, are the real thing, stocked in a 60-foot trout pond or a 65,000-gallon aquarium.

Of course a true Cabela's experience wouldn't be complete without buying something. After all, that's why they're in business. There are things to be found that

you never dreamed existed: field-tested boots for your hunting dog, aqua-glow plastic lizard bait ("lighting up bass for thirty years"), or a camouflage snowsuit for your infant (testimony that "the family who preys together, stays together").

Cabela's grizzlies will greet you at 110 Cabela Boulevard in East Dundee. For more information, call (734) 529–4700 or visit www.cabelas.com.

Cabela's:

An easy-to-find mega-sporting goods store off U.S. 23, with a 48-foot mountain inside the front door.

you know you're in
michigan when...
...celery is your biggest stalker

"The thought of 2,000 people crunching celery all at the same time" may have been horrifying to George Bernard Shaw, but it would have been music to the ears of western Michigan farmers who each year manage the labor-intensive job of growing 2,000 temperamental acres of celery seeds.

Few people realize that muck-enriched Kalamazoo is the North American birthplace of this kissin' cousin to carrots and parsley. In fact, this is one place where being up to your eyeballs in muck is a good thing, since that's just what celery seedlings crave. The muckier the soil, the better the celery.

At one point Michigan exported more than 99 million pounds of celery a year, but competition from year-round producers like California and Florida forced cutbacks, dropping the state's overall production ranking to third.

Yet stalking the halls of the nation's only celery museum has become a pastime for at least 2,000 people annually. Guests at Portage's Celery Flats Interpretive Center (7335 Garden Lane, a quarter-mile east of South Westnedge Avenue in Portage; 269–329–4252) feed on more facts than their celery heart ever imagined. (For example, two stems give you as much potassium as a banana with far fewer calories—only twenty.) Another favorite is the vintage poster advertising Dunkley's Kalamazoo Cherrytone Celery Tonic (containing 20 percent alcohol), claiming that the veggie works as an aphrodisiac.

Celery:

The country's first celery seed was planted in Kalamazoo. Now the city hosts a whole museum dedicated to the crunch heard 'round the world.

you know you're in
michigan when...
...cherry pits are fuel for thought

Eau Claire, Michigan, is home to the International Cherry Pit Spitting Contest. While that's a noble pursuit, what all those competitors don't realize is they're spitting away perfectly good energy. Surprisingly, cherry pits are gaining a reputation as an alternative fuel.

The idea is the brainchild of Chris and Joy Storms of Kingsley, Michigan. Situated in the heart of the state's cherry industry, with a proliferation of canning plants nearby, it seemed a shame for all those pits to go to waste. Fear not! Chris and Joy experimented and found a way to give the discarded pits some respect as a source of heat in pellet stoves.

Their drying and processing technique is a safely guarded secret. (You must be a professional pit processor.... Do not try this at home or you could end up with a batch of moldy stones emitting an everlasting stench.)

Under the name Fire-Pit Pellets, each year they ship roughly 1,320,000 pounds across the United States and as far away as Belgium.

The couple's latest venture is what they call a Pit Pad. Apparently, dried cherry pits have

Cherry Pits:

The cherry's tiniest bit, even the pit, is a precious commodity.

the same properties as a thermos, releasing heat or retaining cold when necessary. After a few minutes in the microwave, a pit-stuffed pad will provide comfort to any bodily pain one might have. They help soothe headaches, backaches, and arthritic conditions, and can even cure a case of cold feet. Put your Pit Pad in the freezer and you've got a personal cooling agent for the hottest of days. When you're feeling in the pits, check out the company's Web site at www.cherrypitstore.com.

Mother Nature apparently does know best.

you know you're in
michigan when...
... fixin's are anything but the pits

Call the Cherry Republic and you'll get a recording that tells you to press a number for a specific department. It goes on to say if you don't like cherries, press six, at which time you're promptly disconnected, a clear indication that life at the Glen Arbor store isn't to be taken too seriously.

President and founder Bob Sutherland kicked off his business in 1989, selling Cherry Republic T-shirts out of the trunk of his car as a way to make money and spread the good news about cherries. In 1993 his product line expanded to include dried cherries and Boomchunka Cookies, made with rolled oats, chunks of chocolate, and, of course, cherries.

From there, his creativity went wild and at last count, a whopping 141 different items help earn the store the title of "World's Largest Exclusive Retailer of Cherries," utilizing more than a million pounds a year. Everything you never imagined with cherries is here: coffee, mustard, ketchup, balsamic vinegar, barbecue sauce, fudge sauce, and BoomChuggaLuggaCherries Soda Pop, to name a few. Cherry salsa remains among the most popular, with 68,004 jars purchased in 2003 alone.

The Cherry Republic retail store (6026 South Lake Street, Glen Arbor) is open seven days a week, 365 days a year. Or visit the Cherry Cafe next door for a taste of homemade delights. Call (800) 206–6949 for more information or catalogue sales, or visit www.cherryrepublic.com (cherry ice cream not available for delivery).

You can take home what some claim to be the world's greatest cherry pie from Beulah's Cherry Hut, a 175-seat family restaurant that began in 1922 as a pie stand. Presently they turn out some 300 pies a day in their eighty-four-pie-capacity ovens. According to the Case family, owners since 1959, the secret is the purity of ingredients: no preservatives and all handmade.

Open from Memorial Day through the third week in October, the Cherry Hut with its hard-to-miss smiley-face red sign sits at 211 North Michigan Highway, U.S. Highway 31, Beulah. For more information call (616) 882–4431 or visit www.cherryhutproducts .com. Mail order is available for their cherry jams and jellies even during the off season.

Cherry Republic:

With its cherry crop, here's proof that Michigan can do anything bigger and better.

you know you're in
michigan when...
...copper lays a golden egg

Travel as far north as you can in Michigan and you'll find yourself in a town suitably named Copper Harbor. In this region of the Keweenaw Peninsula (the part jutting out of the U.P.) sits the greatest collection of copper ore deposits found anywhere in the world.

It seems that prehistoric people were the first to discover Michigan's metal, mining an estimated 1.5 billion pounds between 5000 and 1200 B.C.

But it wasn't until 1842, when the Chippewa ceded all 30,000 square miles of the U.P. to the U.S. government, that the real "Copper Rush" began. Thousands came to gamble on clawing their way to fortunes, much like the state's lottery tickets promise today.

Boomtowns sprang up overnight. Ellis Island was on overload with immigrants seeking directions to Copper Harbor. The nation was becoming electrified, literally, expanding the need for copper to help with this newfangled thing called lighting. Calumet was among the first cities in the world to install electric streetlights and trolley cars.

 Michigan led the nation in copper production, peaking in 1916 at 135 tons. Work was plentiful; life was good. Then the boom went bust. What happened?

> **Copper Mines:**
>
> Reminders of the world's greatest native copper ore deposits, once a booming business in the U.P.

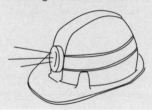

Two people made the difference: Uncle Sam and Henry Ford. In 1921 the government stopped buying copper, and auto plants in Detroit started hiring.

Slowly the mining companies went out of business, and Michigan's last copper mine closed its shaft in 1995.

Thanks to historical pride, a number of mines are now open for tourists seeking the thrill of donning a hard hat and being thrust hundreds of feet below ground into the bowels of a dark mine. It's a family bonding experience better than Disney World.

During the summer months check out Arcadian mine in Hancock, Quincy Mine in Keweenaw, or Adventure Copper Mine off Highway 38 in Greenland. In the winter the mines' dark caves become hibernation homes for thousands of bats.

you know you're in
michigan when...

... it's November 15 and there's not a tradesperson to be seen

Oh, deer... it's November 15. The roof is leaking, the yard needs cleanup, and the toilet's backed up, but there's not a repair person in sight. Most of them have taken to the woods in hot pursuit of big bucks, making those left behind feel as if they're competing on a new reality show, *The Last Vegetarian Standing*.

Michigan's fifteen-day firearms deer hunting season creates a form of feeding frenzy, and not just on venison. It's estimated that three-quarters of a million hunters, mostly men, each shell out $28 for a license to kill. Their prey is the white-tailed deer, aptly named for the white under their tails, flagged when danger is sensed. Only those deer with at least a three-inch-high rack (as in antlers) may be hunted, unless a special license to hunt the antlerless is purchased.

Michigan's deer population has been steadily increasing by 30 to 40 percent a year. At last count (if there's an effective way to count animals that live in forests and brush and don't have to report to the Census Bureau), there were 1.75 million deer, with the majority now living in the Lower Peninsula. About 500,000 will be taken by hunters with firearms, archery, or muzzle loaders.

The most dangerous day of the year is November 14, the day before the season starts—not for the deer, but for the hunters en route. Each year the Michigan Deer Crash Coalition records upwards of 500 car/deer accidents during that single twenty-four-hour period.

No matter what you think of it, hunting is fashionable. One northern Michigan television station even offers viewers the opportunity to display photos of their conquest. You can submit your entry to www.bigol buck.com so the 6:00 news viewers can check out your deer carcass along with their dinner.

Deer Hunting:

November 15 becomes a statewide holiday every year, when hunters begin a two-week excused absence from work.

you know you're in
michigan when...

... it's Thanksgiving and the turkeys take to the field

A Michigan tradition: football and feathers for Thanksgiving. For more than seventy years the Detroit Lions have played an NFL game on Turkey Day. Actually, it's more than just a Michigan tradition: Faithful sports fans all around the country have transformed this annual holiday event into the single most recognized ritual in the history of American sports.

The Thanksgiving Day game started as a move of desperation when the team's first owner, G. A. Richards, had trouble filling the stands despite having a winning season. How do you sell more tickets? His answer: Have the team hurl the pigskin before you slice the turkey breast.

It worked. On November 26, 1934, an over-capacity crowd of 26,000 at the University of Detroit stadium (with thousands more turned away) watched their Lions fall 19–16 to the Chicago Bears. An NFL holy day was born.

At last count the Lions had a Thanksgiving Day record of 33–30–2. They sell out every game, but they're still desperate . . . to win the Big One, or even to play in it. Detroit is one of only seven teams that have never been in the Super Bowl.

True, the Lions have gobbled their way to the brunt of many a joke. As an example, Jay Leno once told his national audience

Detroit Lions Thanksgiving Day Game:

Detroit was the first to play on Thanksgiving; Dallas became copycats twenty years later.

that on Thanksgiving he watched touch football—the Detroit Lions. "Peyton Manning threw four touchdowns yesterday in the win over the Lions. What was the score? 41–9. He did all that while eating a turkey leg."

Michiganians are now getting used to a fairly predictable holiday. . . . Watch the Detroit Thanksgiving Day parade, watch the Lions play, watch the family overeat, and wait for the turkey's sleep-inducing chemical, L-tryptophan, to kick in for a nice, long nap.

19

you know you're in
michigan when...
...a Piston isn't always under the hood of your car

Pistons in Detroit. No, this is not another chronicle on the automotive industry. This story's seeds, in fact, were not even planted in Michigan. At the risk of leaving a bittersweet aftertaste, the truth is that the National Basketball Association's Detroit Pistons are a by-product of Indiana.

The year was 1941 and Fred Zollner, owner of a lucrative auto piston manufacturing plant, put together a short-lived winning basketball team called the Fort Wayne Zollner Pistons. Their mascot was a tin man made of pistons with a Z on his chest, in all probability a mutation of the Wizard of Oz character and Zorro.

In 1957 the team crossed state lines permanently, becoming the Detroit Pistons and beginning their thirty-two-year quest for an NBA championship. Zollner grew impatient and sold the team in 1974 to Bill Davidson, who made millions in auto windshields and even more in sports. His back-to-back Bad Boy champions of 1989 and 1990 (Dennis "Worm" Rodman, Joe Dumars, Rick Mahorn, Bill Laimbeer, Isaiah Thomas, Vinnie "Microwave" Johnson) became good guys of the skies, the first pro franchise with its own "Round Ball One" plane.

Davidson hit the mega-millions jackpot in 2004 with the Pistons NBA championship, his Tampa Bay Lightning's Stanley Cup, and his Detroit Shock's WNBA title. Do you think he bets "0 4" or "2 0 0 4" in the lottery?

Detroit Pistons:

The NBA basketball team never won a championship playing at Detroit's Cobo Arena or Pontiac's cavernous Silverdome. It wasn't until they moved into the $100-million Palace of Auburn Hills that they finally wore the crown two years in a row.

you know you're in
michigan when...
...you're a bit salty

If you said Michiganians are the salt of the earth, you wouldn't be far off. Few people realize that much of the state sits on a huge salt bed, created some 230 million years ago when seawater invaded the Michigan basin, evaporating over centuries. Estimates place 30,000 trillion tons of salt underneath fifty-five counties in the Lower Peninsula.

Long before it was iodized, salt was idolized. Stories have been passed down about how Michigan's Indian tribes would take a twenty-pound slab of venison in trade for a fistful of precious salt. Much like the cost of high technology, salt prices have fallen dramatically, resulting in a double-edged sword: more flavorful food and higher blood pressure.

Early in the twentieth century, Michigan led the nation in salt production, but over time, one by one, the mines closed. Morton Salt Company shut down its Port Huron mine in 1980, leaving Detroit with the state's sole salt shaft.

Detroit's salt mining has been more or less constant since 1906 (with poor economic conditions blamed for the stoppage between 1983 and 1998). The Detroit Salt Company now operates the 1,500 acres some 1,140 feet below the city. You'll have to take our word for it—public tours of the

Detroit Salt Mines:

You can shake, but you can't bake, the "pavement-only" seasoning lying deep under the Motor City.

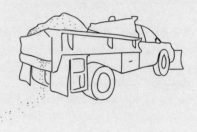

underworld have ceased and the only evidence of their work is at the mineshaft opening located at 12841 Sanders Street in Detroit.

The salt produced here is the type you can see but cannot taste. It's all rock salt, used to deice roadways. And with the harsh Michigan winters, the mine should stay in business for a long time.

... "Bless you, boys" suggests baseball, not a sneeze

Although 1984 was the Chinese Year of the Rat, don't even think of saying that in Michigan or you'll be set straight in a Detroit minute. Clearly the year belonged more to a tiger—as in one of the greatest baseball teams in history, the 1984 World Champion Detroit Tigers.

Their hot streak ignited early. Triumphant in their first nine games, followed by an unprecedented 35–5 record, in the end the Tigers went on to whip the San Diego Padres in the World Series. They joined Babe Ruth's '27 Yankees and Jackie Robinson's '55 Dodgers as only the third team in Major League history to go wire-to-wire (baseball talk for "continuously in first place") and become world champs.

Talk of the Tigers both consumed and unified the entire state. Tiger Stadium attendance went up 25 percent, with a record 2.7 million jamming the stands at Michigan and Trumbull. Then Detroit TV sportscaster Al Ackerman consecrated the team with the words "Bless you, boys," which has stuck like glue ever since.

Engaging personalities filled the dugout, among them Kirk Gibson, Jack Morris, and double-play Hall of Famers Alan Trammell and Lou Whitaker. But none stood out more than the manager, George Lee Anderson, who preferred to be called a more adult-sounding Sparky.

Detroit Tigers:

A baseball team laden with historical superstars, from Ty Cobb to Al Kaline to the "Voice of the Tigers" for forty-two years, announcer Ernie Harwell.

Known for his wacky way with words ("Me carrying a briefcase is like a hot dog wearing earrings"), the former Cincinnati Reds coach went on to become the only manager ever to win a World Series in both the National and American Leagues. Bless you, Sparky.

The Detroit Tigers have moved to their new venue, Comerica Park. If the game isn't as exciting as in the days of the 1984 Bless you boys, you can always spend time riding the baseball Ferris wheel.

you know you're in
michigan when...
...you travel south to Canada—under water

When is the last time you heard of a construction project getting finished a year ahead of schedule? It may have been in 1930, when the Detroit–Windsor Tunnel was a year early in opening.

Just a hundred feet shy of a mile in length, the Detroit–Windsor Tunnel is the "only vehicular international subaqueous border crossing in the world." Translated from fancy schmancy lingo, it means the passageway is the earth's only underwater connection between two nations for cars and trucks.

Respected as one of the great engineering wonders of the world, the passageway, jointly owned by Detroit and Windsor, took just twenty-six months to build, to the tune of $23 million. The two-lane highway (one in each direction) is 22 feet wide and plunges 75 feet under the Detroit River. Claustrophobics will find comfort in 574 lights shining on the 250,000 tiles that line the watertight tubing.

The busy burrow hosts close to 29,000 vehicles a day. Of the nine million crossing a year, 95 percent of them are cars. The tunnel's height of 13 feet 2 inches forces larger trucks to take the scenic route via the Ambassador Bridge.

Worried about gagging on all those exhaust fumes? Fear not. Every minute 1.5 million cubic feet of fresh air is pumped into the tunnel, providing a complete change of air every ninety seconds.

Detroit–Windsor Tunnel:

The tunnel's been providing vehicles with underwater access between the United States and Canada since 1930.

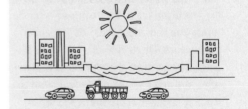

you know you're in
michigan when...
... your dog knows the difference between gee and *haw*

Picture a cross between a cowboy and the driver of a runaway stagecoach on a snow-covered path. Change the image of horses to dogs and there you have the fastest growing sport in Michigan . . . dog sledding.

The thrill of mushing a 6–8–10–20 dog team has reached addictive proportions, particularly in Alger County, where the people population is 9,767 and the dog count is around 5,000. Not a shocking figure, considering that fanatical families each have thirty to forty extra mouths to feed. And those huskies are fussy about their road kill. Beaver and duck are high on their list, but they say "no thanks" to skunk (too rich for their tummies and not good for their breath).

Lest you think that mushers merely go with the flow, think again. Tough physical stamina is required to stand in back, as the leader of the pack, racing 18 miles through the woods on a midnight madness run that takes you into the next morning. Part of the winning equation is the strategy used to schedule mutually agreeable feeding, watering, and bathroom breaks for overly sensitive noses and bladders.

Some of the sport's devotees have opened their sleds to anyone who wants to learn the *gee* (turn right) and *haw* (turn left) of mushing. As expert sledder Ellen Robison says, there are three basic principles to

Dog Sledding:

A manufacturing mecca for dog sleds, Michigan also hosts the U.P. 200, one of the qualifying races for the Iditarod.

remember: "Never let go. Never let go. Never let go. You let go and you're walking home." Ellen and her husband, Dave, are owners of Superior Dog Sleds in Chatham, shipping their quality handmade racing sleds to places as far away as Switzerland. For more info about "drive-them-yourself" tours, contact them at (906) 439–5835 or www.superiordogsleds.com.

you know you're in
michigan when...
...a dream cruise means a ride in an old car

Only one thing gives two million people a reason to line 16 miles of hallowed pavement in the suburbs of Detroit: a car. Well, not just one car; more like 30,000 vintage and custom vehicles all cruisin' down Woodward Avenue, the main drag separating east-siders from west-siders.

The third Saturday in August is an automotive junkie's dream, a chance to relive the glory days of muscle cars and hot rods. The Woodward Dream Cruise is a marathon party paying homage to America's love affair with the automobile, when poodle skirts come out of the closet and guys slick back whatever hair they may have left.

In 1994, Ferndale plumber Nelson House became the godfather of the cruise when he was looking for an innovative way to raise funds for his child's soccer team. An unlikely solution, the cruise gathers funds by selling sponsorships. Driving your vehicle down the street is free.

Almost anything can be classified as a "classic"—loosely defined by the committee as a vehicle that "creates a feeling of nostalgia, stimulates a memory, or fulfills a fantasy." That's why you'll see a host of 50s and 60s T-birds and Barracudas alongside a 2005 goal-of-a-lifetime Viper. They all cruise the strip, over and over and over again.

Auto fans in their lawn chairs get into the action by throwing water on the road, encouraging the old-timers to rev it and burn rubber, or overheat, whichever comes first. The fun and fumes are, pardon the pun, exhausting.

To make the scene complete, nostalgic rock-and-rollers like Freddy "Boom Boom" Cannon, Fabian Forte, and Chubby Checker join those who still remember them to sing, dance, and enjoy riding bumper-to-bumper into the sunset. For more information visit www.woodwarddreamcruise.com

Dream Cruise:

A 16-mile parade of vintage cars vrooming through eight Detroit suburbs.

you know you're in
michigan when...
...the manhole cover tells you so

Walk down the streets of any major city in America, find the first manhole cover you come to, stare at it for a bit, and chances are you'll find the fashionable logo *EJIW*. This stamp indicates it was brought to life in East Jordan, Michigan.

It gives us comforting satisfaction here to know that when the likes of superstars George Clooney and Julia Roberts step their precious feet on a sewer cover in Los Angeles, a Michiganian from East Jordan Iron Works touched it first.

East Jordan (located slightly above the first knuckle on Michigan's geographic ring finger) has been unofficially dubbed the "sewer cover capital of the world." Thanks go to the Malpass family, fourth-generation ironworks owners, who have been making East Jordan a haven for street castings (a kinder, gentler term) since 1883.

Customized covers are their latest offering. Send them a design and your city's slogan and soon you could see something like "Cassapolis—The Perch Capital of Michigan" capping off your neighborhood manholes.

It's hard for a business to survive for decades on one product. So the product line has expanded to include the equally glamorous water works valves and fire hydrants, also distributed worldwide.

East Jordan Iron Works:

A manufacturing plant earning its home town the title Sewer Cover Capital of the World.

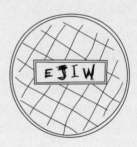

East Jordan Iron Works are also master merchandisers, with the Web site's company store (www.ejiw.com) offering fans the chance to buy anything from an EJIW tie clip or Swiss army knife to an EJIW jacket or beach towel. Who knows, they just might be ready for prime time. Maybe the Home Shopping Network has an opening.

you know you're in
michigan when...
...you use soda pop instead of lipstick

Ben and Jerry, ice cream flavor mavens: meet Ben and Perry, rulers of the world of soda pop flavors. Today their kingdom is known as Faygo, one word representing forty-nine different savory soft drinks. Slobbering down all varieties in one sitting easily qualifies you for a stint on *Fear Factor.*

Ben and Perry Feigenson were Russian immigrant bakers who, in 1907, started marketing beverages out of the back of their horse-drawn wagon. Inspired by their cake frosting recipes, the top finger-licking flavors emerged as Fruit Punch, Strawberry, and Grape.

In the 1960s strawberry was officially changed to Redpop, with a color so powerful it could (and does) put stains on your carpet or lips for months.

With the pipeline supercharged with ideas, the research department is on overload to keep the twenty million bottles and cans produced weekly filled successfully to the brim. Among the enterprising failures were a wine-flavored pop labeled Chateaux Faygeaux, and Royal Hawaiian Pineapple Orange, which proved to be an explosive disaster when the caps flung off, the bottles shattered, and employees ran for their lives.

Faygo pop may be the only company where the commercials have become more famous than the merchandise itself. In the 1970s Faygo's catchy "Remember When You Were a Kid" recorded by Gildersleeve (another one-name wonder, like Eminem) sold more than 75,000 copies, putting it at number three on the pop music chart. Credit can also be given to a long-standing phrase in American lingo, when Herkimer the bottle blower was "too pooped to participate" until he drank Faygo.

But the ultimate memory has to be of the Faygo Kid, who rhythmically asked "Which way did he go? Which way did he go? He went for Faaaaaaaaygooooooooooo!" makes anyone want to go for a bottle of Diet Key Lime Pie.

Faygo Pop:

A beverage institution, as well known for its sing-along commercials as for its soda pop.

...a sauna is the "Finnishing" touch

Welcome to the Upper Peninsula. The first people you'll likely meet are Eino, Toivo, or perhaps an occasional Bruce. Unusual sounding, vowel-ending names are representative of Michigan's king-size Finnish population. Word is that the U.P. has more Finnish folk than cars.

Between 1850 and 1920 communities worked diligently to make the thousands of newcomers feel at home. But it wasn't until 1962 that Negaunee's WLUC TV6 went on the air with the country's only Finnish-language program, *Finland Calling*. More than forty years later, the program is still going strong with original host Carl Pellonpaa enchanting his fellow Finns every Sunday while station technicians don't understand a word he's saying.

The rest of the state can be grateful that the Finnish introduced us to dry heat, used to open the pores and eliminate toxins through sweat while we enjoy mental and physical relaxation in a wooden room. In other words, a sauna. Some say it's more therapeutic than a psychiatrist.

The word *sauna* is properly pronounced "SOW-nah." Think sweating female pig. The Michiganized version is "SAW-nah." A true sauna experience includes jumping in the snow naked between "heats," but if that's not possible, a cold shower will do. The

Finnish Sauna:

In Michigan, people define *fun* as sitting in a heated wooden room, followed by a roll in the snow.

effect can best be summed up in the words of Michigan's only Finnish reggae band, Conga Se Menne:

> Come-a come-a come-a come-a-
> take a sauna with me
> We'll let the steam go
> And yump in the snow
> It'll be much easier if I hit you with
> a cedar bough
> It makes the blood flow. . . .

Some non-Finnish parents fear that saunas are the breeding ground for sexual activity, to which the Finnish respond, "You behave in a sauna like you behave in a church." But how many people attend church wrapped in a towel?

Smorgasbords of fins lie deep in Michigan's great and small lakes, waiting for fisher-women and fishermen to sink their hooks into them. Part of the state's lure to the sport, especially if you're not into opening the refrigerator to thread a slimy, wiggly worm as bait, is that it's the one place where it's legal to fish by hook, net, fly, or spear.

Fly fishing enthusiasts head to the many blue-ribbon trout streams, while inland lakes dish up selections of perch, bluegill, pike, bass, and crappie. (The American Crappie Association swears they're tasty.)

Cheboygan's Black Lake is home to the mysteriously inaccessible sturgeon, an 8-foot-long, 200-pound swimming dinosaur. Since 1948 spear-wielding crowds have waited days for a chance to win the right to harpoon one of five every February. When the quintet has been captured, sturgeon-fishing season is over; whether it's been twelve days or thirty-five minutes.

Each species has its favorite of the Great Lakes. Together the fish add up to a mess of heart-healthy eating: salmon, perch, wall-eye, smelt, and whitefish—the latter two good finds for netters. Don't pass up the opportunity to order fresh Michigan white-fish off a menu for a genuine taste-of-the-state experience.

Occasionally, even aquatic life needs a lift to travel upstream. That's where Michigan's numerous fish ladders come in. One of the best ladder viewings is Grand Rapids' Fish Ladder Park at 560 Front Avenue, NW (616–456–3696), featuring an artistic sculpture that fish jump up on during their seasonal migration.

Fishing:

Every day, on any body of water in the state, you'll see someone sitting, standing, or walking (across frozen water) with a pole in his or her hand.

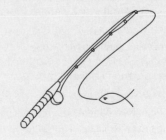

you know you're in
michigan when...
...mail is delivered by pail

E-mail . . . . Snail mail . . . . Sail mail. Applause goes to Michigan's seafaring *J. W. Westcott II,* the only boat delivering mail to moving freighters, for coining the latter of these terms years before that ubiquitous voice first spewed out "You've Got Mail."

Water is a way of life here, and waterways have requisites unto themselves. Captain J. W. Westcott recognized that in 1895 when he made the first "mail-by-the-pail delivery" to ships passing through the Detroit River on their way to the Great Lakes. That year 46,994 pieces of mail were dropped into the bucket and hoisted onto some 19,000 ships. The following twelve months saw a 400 percent rise in business.

Gradually the Great Lakes fleet dwindled to 150 vessels. To stay afloat, the sailing post office, with its own 48222 zip code, launched pilot exchanging services so that each ship on the Detroit River could have a registered United States or Canadian pilot on-board.

During what appeared to be a routine pilot exchange to a Norwegian freighter in October 2001, rough seas sank the 45-foot-long *J. W. Westcott II,* leaving two of its own crew members dead. The *J. W.,* originally built in 1949, was raised, refurbished, and back on the job in six months. Today the oldest floating post office remains steadfast in its conviction to deliver the mail in wind,

Floating Post Office:

The *J. W. Westcott II* is the only floating post office with its own zip code, offering round-the-clock delivery service of mail-in-a-pail.

rain, snow, or sleet mid-April through December.

Like so many other things, the mail isn't what it used to be. Among the 6,000 annual ship-to-ship deliveries have been pets, televisions, golf clubs, a 3-foot-long frozen tuna, and a dozen Domino's pizzas.

The *J. W. Westcott II* can be found at its Detroit home base at the foot of Twenty-fourth Street, just west of the Ambassador Bridge.

Have a seat at Miller's Bar on Michigan Avenue in Dearborn (or, as the locals say it, "Deerburn"), wait thirty seconds, and then ask the person next to you where he or she works. It's a good bet your companion will answer "Fords." You may have to wait a few minutes as you get farther from Dearborn to get the same answer; but be trusting, you will get it. People throughout all of Michigan either work at or know someone who works at "Fords."

Truth of the matter is, no one works at "Fords." There is no such place as Fords, but everyone in the state says that there is. They habitually take a proper noun—in this case, Ford—and add the letter s to make it sound like a plural, when in reality it's a possessive.

This quirky practice has been going on for decades, since the Ford Motor Company hired employees for the first manufacturing assembly line. It took far too much time and energy to say one worked on "Ford's assembly line," so the abbreviated version for place of employment became simply "Fords."

The erroneous possessive malaprop has been driving English teachers crazy ever since, expanding to include other Michigan home-based companies, with or without assembly lines, like Chrysler (Chryslers),

Kmart (Kmarts), and Meijer, originally Meijer Thrifty Acres (Meijers).

While Michiganians add an s to other industries, like saying they're going to Krogers, a shortened form of Kroger's supermarket, you'll never hear them say they're going to Mobils or Shells when in need of a fill-up. Seems they want to distance themselves as much as possible when it comes to taking ownership of any form of gas.

Fords:

"Working at Fords" has become a common example of Michigan's use and misuse of possessive nouns.

you know you're in
michigan when...
...fudgies take over the island

The mandatory first stop on any trip to Mackinac Island is to one of the thirteen fudge shops lining Main Street so you can earn your "fudgie" badge. Here, fudge-making is a mouth-watering entertainment experience, watching the thick, gooey, hot fudge being poured on marble slabs to cool as an attendant jokes with the crowd of ravenous onlookers.

Fudge has been synonymous with the island since 1887, when carpenter Newton James Murdick, like any good son, wanted others to share his mother's fabulous fudge recipe. The Grand Hotel opened that same year, creating an influx of hungry newcomers. It was a natural combination, and the fudgie race was on.

Other fudge shops soon opened, each now alleging to be the oldest, original, most famous, or best, even though culinary experts say they're hard to tell apart. All the confections include butter and sugar blended with extras like mint, cranberries, or peanut butter to come up with twenty or so variations on "plain Jane" chocolate.

And they all sell tons—thirty or forty tons per store. Even the hikers along the 8-mile trail around the island are all carrying the calorie-laden little white boxes with the plastic knives inside.

Fudgie:

(FUH-jee). Noun. One of the thousands of tourists visiting Mackinac Island each summer day, mostly to consume a sweet, chocolate confection known as fudge, either by purchasing half-pound slabs or snatching handfuls of free samples.

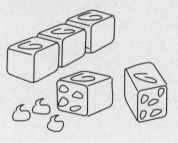

FYI: your nose isn't playing tricks on you. The smell of Mackinac Island fudge is in the air, thanks to fans blowing the scent through the windows onto the streets. This serves as a resourceful marketing tool and a cover-up for the other "fudge" horses have dropped on the street.

you know you're in
michigan when...
...ice trees replace snowmen

Kids in Michigan grow up on a winter recreation diet of tumbling in the snow while flapping their arms to make angel wings or forming snowmen with charcoal belly buttons. As maturity sets in, a more sophisticated form of those arctic antics becomes necessary.

Meet the Ice Tree—Gaylord's answer to Rockefeller Center.

Every year for more than six decades, the city has erected a three-story metal structure, resembling something between a tripod and a pyramid, on the front lawn of the City/County Building.

Personifying the configuration, let's say it next receives a colonoscopy of sorts, using a long pipe that runs to the top and remains there. When it gets really, really cold (say, anytime beginning in August), a 24/7 shower goes to work, spraying a nice, even trickle for months. Although not a pretty picture at first, ice eventually begins to form, manifesting in layers upon layers of beautifully frozen prisms.

Mother Nature can't guarantee uniformity, but each year the tree glaciates to about 20 feet with a girth of 22 feet, weighing in at an estimated 245 tons.

Yes, the tree has fallen down a couple of times, almost hitting the judge's office.

But then, what would you expect if you've had 273,000 gallons of water thrown on you? An expensive water bill? Surprisingly for the entire season, the tree—water and all—costs under $200.

Gaylord Ice Tree:

A hot shower (cold water takes longer to freeze) becomes a free-form ice tree on the forty-fifth parallel.

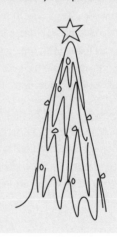

33

you know you're in
michigan when...
...baby's first words are "strained peas, please"

Only in Michigan could strained peas be the genesis for a billion-dollar food company. It happened in Fremont in 1927, when Dorothy Gerber sought a quick solution for her infant's nutritional shortcomings and found it in the existing family business. Fremont Canning Company, an adult fruit and vegetable cannery, soon became the answer to her peeling, steaming, scraping, and straining prayers.

Reinventing itself as Gerber Products Company, the corporation began pushing out pureed peas and prunes, improving the quality of life for moms and their babies all across America. Today their product line has grown to include anything a little one's heart and bottom could desire, from life insurance to diaper rash ointment.

Fremont continues to celebrate its roots with the National Baby Food Festival, a five day kitsch-fest giving adults the opportunity to do things they never dreamed they'd do while sober.

The baby-food-eating contest pairs two-person bib-linked teams, simultaneously feeding each other five jars of baby food, to see who's the quickest and neatest. The team with the least amount of spillage wins. An epicurean's nightmare, the baby food cook-off requires chefs to create an original recipe using at least one jar of pureed spinach or something equally gourmet.

Gerber Baby Foods:

Each year Fremont's manufacturing plant produces millions of jars of strained fruits, vegetables, and anything else the toothless can swallow.

And to put the rumors to rest . . . the original Gerber baby was not Elizabeth Taylor or Brooke Shields. It was Ann Turner Cook, now an author, living in Florida.

For the most up-to-date National Baby Food Festival info, contact their headquarters at 7 East Main Street, Fremont, MI 49412, (231) 924–2270, or their Web site with the countdown to festival time at www.baby foodfest.com.

you know you're in
michigan when...

...you're surrounded by six quadrillion gallons of water

One of the first things every schoolchild in Michigan learns is that the word *homes* represents more than comfy habitats lining a neighborhood street. HOMES is a cutesy acronym enabling one to quickly recall the names of all five of the Great Lakes: Huron, Ontario, Michigan, Erie, and Superior.

Given that Michigan's primary nickname is "The Great Lakes State" because it touches four of the five Great Lakes, knowing that acronym alone could make the difference in passing or failing the fourth grade or a state government job interview.

Collectively, the Great Lakes are the largest surface of fresh water—more than 94,000 square miles—anywhere on earth. We have more water than they have land in the states of New York, New Jersey, Connecticut, Rhode Island, Massachusetts, Vermont, and New Hampshire combined. Wherever you are in Michigan, you're never more than 85 miles away from *H, O, M, E,* or *S.*

Where there's water, there's shoreline, and with 3,288 miles we naturally have more of that than anyone else, too. Imagine a stretch of shore running all the way from Maine to Florida contained in just one state, surrounding us like a drought-protective halo.

Lake Erie is the smallest. Lake Superior, once called *Kitchi-gummi* (Chippewa for "great water"), is the largest and deepest.

Forty miles off Munising, Lake Superior bottoms out at 1,332 feet. You could take one of the tallest buildings in the world, Chicago's Sears Tower, plop it down there, and only a few floors would be sticking out of the water.

Speaking of names, we can thank the British for Lake Michigan, a derivative of the Indian word *Michigami,* meaning "large lake." Much better than the French-designed maps of the mid-1600s that labeled Lake Michigan *Lac des Puans,* the "lake of the stinking people."

Great Lakes:

One-fifth of the world's fresh surface water, if spread out the Great Lakes would submerge the United States under 9½ feet of water.

Ask anyone where to satisfy your penchant for pierogies or where you might learn to polka, and they'll immediately answer: "Hamtramck." It's Michigan's answer to a cross between Warsaw and the Lawrence Welk Show.

A plethora of anything Polish can be found within the 2.1-square-mile city. But it wasn't always that way.

The French were the first to settle here in 1798, and while everyone thinks of Hamtramck as Polish, the word itself is not. A French Revolutionary War hero, Col. Jean Francois Hamtramck, is the city's namesake.

If it weren't for John and Horace Dodge, the city might still be munching on croissants and crepes. On June 10, 1910, ground was broken for their Dodge Brothers Motor Car Company at the intersection of Joseph Compeau (another Frenchman) and Conant Streets.

Polish immigrants soon flocked to work at the auto company, swelling the city's population from 3,589 to 46,615 between 1910 and 1920. In fact, that explosive growth rate gave Hamtramck the distinction of being the fastest growing-community in the United States.

The first auto produced in Hamtramck rolled off the line on November 14, 1914, when the city now known as "Pole Town"

Hamtramck:

Originally a Polish enclave, the city has gained national recognition for its publicly announced Islamic call to prayer and a 30-foot-tall kielbasa.

was unofficially named Dodge City. The Polish cowboys carried the theme so far as to bring in, as guest honor for the week, none other than Roy Rogers.

The years have changed Hamtramck, the only city completely bordered by Detroit. Now a melting pot with forty-seven different ethnicities, you'll still hear the oom pah pahs, but you'll also hear the Islamic call to prayer broadcast five times a day over the city's public address system.

The visual signs of the Polish influence remain. Stroll down Holbrook Avenue and you can't miss the Kowalski Company's sign, hanging since 1950, a time before we cared about cholesterol and bigger *was* better. Your eyes are not deceiving you; it's a 30-foot-tall neon kielbasa being stabbed by two fork tines, a sight made even more attractive after downing a few brewskis.

...you can honestly say you've been to Hell and back

The next time someone tells you to go to Hell, do yourself a favor and take them up on it. "A small town on the way up," it's here you'll find what Hell on Earth is really like—or at least Hell in Michigan, the only city in the United States with the damned name.

The town was founded in 1841 by Catskill Mountains transplant George Reeve, who, in a heated argument over the name, finally shouted out, "You can call it *Hell* for all I care." It's now in the fiendish hands of John Colone, a former auto dealership owner.

Colone, as major hellion, is the owner of Screams Ice Cream from Hell and Halloween, where the main attraction is the Sundae Bar scooped out of an authentic 1810 coffin from Transylvania. The luscious toppings all have nauseous names like *bat droppings* (chocolate chips), *ghost poop* (mini marshmallows), and *buttersnot* (butterscotch). You're on your own for toenail clippings and petrified gallstones.

Colone also holds the deed to the Hell Country Store and Spirits, with its official U.S. Postal Outlet attracting hordes of happy customers on April 15 to receive the official "Taxes from Hell" postmark.

Besides the roughly 200 residents (numbers change daily), the bona fide U.S. Weather Station here gives meteorologists an ideal opportunity to use their "When Hell freezes over" line.

The latest industry here is Greetings from Hell, producing cards appropriate for almost any occasion, but especially good for weddings. Here's a sampling from one of their get-well missives:

> The gang at work was worried sick about your ill condition
> And so they sent me to a store upon a get-well mission
> This pretty card, this special dirt are supposed to make you well
> At least that's what the people said when I was there in Hell.

The accompanying bottle of "Dirt from Hell" is labeled as "freshly unearthed soil from Hell, slow roasted to regulatory perfection and bottled while it's still warm." Sure to make even a well person feel just a bit sicker.

Hell:

A great place to take first-time visitors for a Helluva good time.

Apologies to Bill Shakespeare, his famous quotation, "That which we call a rose by any other name would smell as sweet" would be translated in Michigan to "a melon by a name other than *Howell* would not be as sweet."

Back in the 1920s farmers in Howell came up with a distinctive blend of muskmelon, patented as a Howell Honey Sweet but often referred to as a Howell Honey Rock. It may look like a cantaloupe, but don't say that too loud. There really is a difference.

Howell's honey rocks are undeniably the biggest, juiciest, sweetest melons you've ever seen. How big are their melons? The soccer-ball-sized melons weigh around five pounds each, making them larger than a cantaloupe, sweeter than a honeydew, and, at 90 percent H_2O, almost as juicy as a watermelon.

Every crop-producing community in Michigan has a festival to tout its fruits and vegetables. No surprise here that during prime pickin' time, at the end of each August, Howell's melons take center stage, attracting an appreciative audience of more than 60,000.

The Howell Melon Festival has grown from a farmer's market in 1959 to a multifaceted affair for the whole family, with a slew of

Howell Melons:

No melons on the planet are bigger, sweeter, or juicier than those named for the city that made them famous.

activities and the obligatory melon tent. Don't miss the original-recipe Howell melon ice cream, which took first place in the dairy category at the Michigan State Fair in 1960.

It's a shame these treasures can't be shared with the rest of the nation. The skin of a Howell melon is so thin that they're all but impossible to ship, proving it really does pay to have thick skin.

you know you're in
michigan when...
...Hush Puppies are "sole" food

Leave it to a Michigan company to make sense out of a fried dough ball, barking dogs, and pigskin. Wolverine World Wide has been doing business in Rockford since 1888, but it wasn't until the 1950s, when the United States government approached the tannery to devise an effective use for pigskin, that their famous Hush Puppies shoes took shape.

Post-World War II, America's aching feet were strapped into high heels or laced into wing tips, screaming for casual style and relief. Enter the pigskin comfort shoe.

Peddling the anonymous shoe in Tennessee, a curious salesman was served a dinner of catfish and the deep-fried cornmeal dough balls known as *hush puppies*. Turns out the hush puppies did just what the name implies . . . throw a barking dog a hush puppy, and the animal silences immediately.

A light bulb went off in the salesman's mind. "Barking dogs" was an idiom for sore feet. His shoes were the remedy. Aha! From that moment on, the pigskin liberators would be known as Hush Puppies.

Today Hush Puppies are sold in 115 countries. Every day, somewhere in the world, more than twenty-six pairs a minute find new soles to save.

Every shoe box bears the brand's popular trademark, a droopy-eared, sad-eyed Bassett hound whose massive feet look as if they've been dog-tired for years.

Hush Puppies:

A brand of casually chic pigskin shoes today popularized by celebrities like Brooke Shields and Harry Connick Jr.

you know you're in
michigan when...
...sailors welcome the first freeze

The saying goes, "When life gives you lemons, make lemonade." In Michigan that means "When winter gives you ice, make ice boats."

The first ice boat prototype in the state, basically a sail-powered sled, popped up in 1886 on Gull Lake near Kalamazoo. Those working in lumber camps picked up on the ice-boating idea to break the monotony during the brutal winters. During the Depression, before the advent of television and video games, it also became a popular spectator sport, attracting crowds along Lake St. Clair. But it wasn't until 1936, when master shipbuilder Archie Arroll relocated to Detroit from Scotland, that ice yachting stood on solid ground, in a manner of speaking.

Working in the *Detroit News* hobby shop, Arroll created the DN 60 (*DN* stands for *Detroit News,* 60 represents the size of the sail).

Today DN ice boats remain the most popular in the world. The International DN Ice Yacht Racing Association—founded on Oakland County's Cass Lake in 1953—now boasts thousands of members worldwide.

Michigan's Ron Sherry, three-time World Champion in the DN class and himself a boat builder, says the world's fastest non-

Ice Boating:

The fastest sport powered by Mother Nature. The fame of Detroit's ice boats has crossed the Atlantic.

motor sport gives you a thrill unlike anything else. Maneuvering three times around two markers set 1 mile apart, the acceleration causes sailors to experience a feeling of g-force as they head toward the record 148 miles per hour.

Not an activity to try on thin ice. As Sherry claims, "It's the most fun you can have with your clothes on."

you know you're in
michigan when...
...your tip up tips down

Looking out over a frozen Michigan lake, one notices something peculiar: sticks seemingly growing out of the ice, some bobbing silently, others whistling. These are the tip ups, ice-fishing devices triggering a whipping action when a sucker's on the line.

Multiple lines are a perk for putting up with the cold, but juggling them all would be a little like operating a marionette. That's where numerous tip ups pay off. Set out a string of them; wait for the red flag to go down or the bells and whistles to sound; grab the pole; and reel 'em in.

Houghton Lake may be the state's most popular ice-fishing spot—if not for its stock of pike, walleye, and bass, then for its sheer size alone. At 22,000 shallow acres, it's Michigan's largest inland lake, providing plenty of room to prop up one's fishing shanty before sawing a two-by-four, the most common size for an ice hole.

A typical winter weekend will see thousands of tip ups. Even more of them surface on the January weekend known as Tip Up Town, a festival for cold-blooded folks who love the thrill of riding a tilt-a-whirl when it's ten below.

But some sports are better saved for the arctic air. Take for instance, turkey bowling.

The rules are simple.... Carve a 30-foot alley in the ice. Place real bowling pins at one end. Pick up a ten-pound frozen turkey and hurl it down, hoping to score a strike. For the children's version, use a frozen chicken.

Ice Fishing:

When the lakes freeze, the fishing faithful take to the ice 24/7 for a chance to catch the big one.

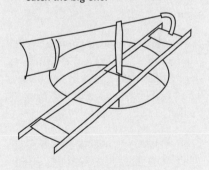

...summer camp means ballet, oboe, and Shakespeare

What does the unlikely trio of Mike Wallace, Norah Jones, and Cathy Guisewite have in common? They were all once students at Interlochen Arts Academy, Michigan's equivalent to Juilliard in a woodsy neighborhood.

What would make a kid beg to sit in class in an eighty-degree hut without air conditioning? To be totally immersed in their craft amid glacial lakes and pensive pines.

Located just outside of Traverse City (around the first knuckle on Michigan's pinkie), this breathtaking 1,200-acre campus and its plethora of artsy activities persuade kids from all fifty states and thirty-eight foreign countries to trek here each summer.

Interlochen first opened its tents in 1928 with only three classes and 115 students. The summer staff alone now numbers more than 1,000. Attendees are more than double that.

Today Interlochen is recognized as the premier site for right-brain-dominant young people: dancers, singers, actors, writers, visual artists. And it's not just for summer any more.

In 1962, a year-round academy began, the nation's first independent high school dedicated to the arts.

While full-time students receive an academic education as well, the life of a summer camper is focused and disciplined: practice, perform, practice, and perform. Some 265,000 visitors annually witness the works of the notable knicker-clad campers (maybe Mike Wallace had better knees when he was eight). Interlochen's presentations are like multivitamins. With an annual schedule of 750 concerts, you could easily take in more than one a day.

The list of famous alumni is extensive, and includes: singing sensation Josh Groban; actress Felicity (*Desperate Housewives*) Huffman; Google co-founder and president Larry Page; and Playboy Enterprise CEO and president Christie Hefner.

Interlochen Arts Academy:

A summer camp gone year-round, where some of America's elite received their cultural training.

you know you're in
michigan when...
...cherries are more than a-pie-in-the-sky celebration

Life in Michigan is more than just a bowl of cherries: it's more than 40,000 acres of cherries, producing some 300 million pounds each year of tart and sweet.

While some may complain that the weather in Michigan is the pits, the cherry tree couldn't be happier here, with brisk Lake Michigan winds maintaining a frigid winter and a cool summer. More than 75 percent of all tart cherries in the United States are grown in the state, mainly in the northwest portion, earning Traverse City the title of "Cherry capital of the world." Even the airport is named Cherry National.

That's why every July more than half a million people converge on the productive town for an eight-day fete of cherry activities. The celebration started in 1926 as the "Blessing of the Blossoms" and grew so rapidly that in 1931 the state passed a resolution making it a gala on the same scale as Mardi Gras and the Rose Parade.

Of course there's food, plenty of it, in every shape, size, and food group a cherry can withstand. One year the Cherry Festival Queen gingerly transported a fifty-pound cherry pie to the White House.

This must be the most amazing celebration in the country. At least that's what the Food Network said in 2003, when it picked the

Irresistible Cherry Festival:

Traverse City is all cherries all the time, even more so (if that's possible) during July's annual celebration.

National Cherry Festival as the number one Top Amazing Celebration for the year.

Every other year the Blue Angels perform their stunts high above Grand Traverse Bay. It's the one time you don't want to stand too close to the show; blown-out eardrums and a major neck cramp could result.

While the festival goes on rain or shine, hot or cold, the cherries don't. On at least one occasion poor farming weather forced "Michigan's" cherry festival crop to be flown in from Washington State. For more information on the shindig, check out www.cherryfestival.org or call (231) 947–4230.

A haven for nature lovers, Isle Royale sits 20 miles off the northwestern coast of the Upper Peninsula, or about a 4½-hour ferry boat ride from Copper Harbor. Surrounded by the treacherous waters of Lake Superior, the 210 square miles of pristine wilderness can be reached safely only by ferry boats and seaplanes.

Once there, you'll encounter 165 miles of scenic hiking trails and perhaps a wild animal or two. On any given day there will be far more animals than people in the park, though you won't see any bears, bobcats, coyotes, or chipmunks. Isle Royale is home to the highest density of moose in the world. With a herd of 1,100, that averages about five moose per square mile.

The park is officially open only from April through October, yet a team led by Michigan Technological University's Rolf Peterson has fought the elements in the dead of winter to learn more about what goes on with our four-legged friends. It's also the site of the world's longest continuously running wildlife research project. Since 1958 investigators have been searching to understand the role wolves play in the year-to-year fluctuations of the moose population.

It's not always a pretty picture. The wolves, numbering annually between nineteen and twenty-nine, use the moose as their main source of sustenance, preying primarily on calves. On the other hand, moose, which in Algonquin means "twig eater," are vegetarians. Imagine bulking up as they do on nothing but salad, sans the dressing.

Researchers believe the moose swam to Isle Royale in 1912. Wolves made the trek over the ice around 1950. And the two species have been attempting to coexist ever since.

Dozens of campgrounds and the eleven-room Rock Harbor Inn play host to the summer tourists. If you're in search of excellent fishing and beautiful surroundings, Isle Royale is a place you simply "moose" visit. For more information visit www.isle.royale.national-park.com or call (906) 482–0984.

Isle Royale National Park:

An island sanctuary housing more moose and wolves than people.

Keweenaw County, also referred to as the Keweenaw Peninsula, is as far north as you can go in Michigan. It's also the least populated county. Jetting out of the very tip of the U.P., like a cowlick on one's head, this is a place where the winters are harsh and long.

Not an easy place to live, unless you're in search of a monastic lifestyle. That's exactly what two graduates of the University of Michigan were looking for when they settled in Eagle Harbor in 1983.

Affiliating with the Byzantine Church, the two new monks did what everyone in the Keweenaw (as the area is commonly called) said could never be done: they built an 11,000-square-foot monastery and a thriving business.

Granted, their success did not come overnight. Years of dedicated 5-to-9 workdays—that's 5:00 A.M to 9:00 P.M.—played a major part. The other credits go to prayer and thimbleberries.

Conquering both bears and poison ivy, Fathers Basil and Nicholas passionately picked the dainty thimbleberries—a fragile wild fruit, similar to a jumbo raspberry and related to the blackberry—transforming them into an incredibly flavorful jam. And as the saying goes, "the rest is fruitful history."

Jampot:

Two monks started a thriving gourmet jam business on not much more than a berry and a prayer.

Word spread quickly. Customers and donations poured in. Even a few more monks joined them.

Today the Jampot, open May through October with year-round mail order, keeps The Society of St. John in the black with offerings of jams, chocolate truffles, and cakes. A real winner is their Abbey Cake filled with raisins and pecans, all "liberally laced with Jack Daniel's."

Cold temperatures aside, boundless beauty survives in this area all four seasons, with magnificent landscapes and glorious shorelines. Clearly divine intervention allowed humans to see what the thimbleberries knew all along: This place really is Heaven on Earth.

The best way to reach the monks is through the Internet: www.societystjohn.com.

Name a Michigan company that has become a marketing marvel, watching one million of its products fly off the shelves every day without ever spending a dime on advertising. Yes, Madison Avenue would kill for the secret behind the Chelsea Milling Company and its little blue box, affectionately known as Jiffy Mix.

The story began in 1930, predating both Betty Crocker and Martha Stewart, when Mabel White Holmes laid eyes on a boy eating a homemade biscuit that looked like a hybrid hockey puck and gum eraser. Acting on a childhood memory of the family cook ordering her to "Tell your father them good, hot biscuits will be ready in a jiffy," Mabel concocted a quick 'n' easy prepared biscuit mix, giving birth to the home baking mix market.

The dough was quick to rise (pardon the irresistible pun), to what today is a $2-billion industry. The eighteen-carat product line features gut-busting goodies like cakes, frostings, muffins, and all-purpose mix, which at one point outsold the highly commercialized Bisquick mix.

Maybe a viable alternative to Michigan's motto "If you seek a pleasant peninsula, look around you" is "Be prepared, be reasonable, and be ready in a jiffy."

Chelsea Milling Company gives weekday tours, with samples, of its all-purpose milling and packaging facility. Call (734) 475–1361 and ask for Tour Scheduling or check out www.jiffymix.com.

Jiffy Mix:

The tower of the Chelsea Milling Company is a 23-foot-by-50-foot exact replica of its famous blue box, so from anywhere in town you can spot them "in a Jiffy."

you know you're in
michigan when...
...litter becomes a "purrrfect" discovery

Great ideas all start someplace. Every cat-loving household can thank Michigan for the ingenious concept that sprang out of Cassopolis (almost to Michigan's geographical wrist, down below the pinkie).

Take one messy feline, one whiney woman, one dogged man, and you have all the trappings for what was to become a golden egg.

It's 1947. Kay Draper is sick and tired of her cat's paws tracking sawdust and ashes all over the house. Isn't there someone who could come up with a neater idea for furnishing a kitty's box?

Enter Ed Lowe, who recently returned to Cassopolis after a stint in the Navy, to become an industrial absorbent salesman. His suggestion of clay saved the day for Kay and her cat.

A light bulb went on in Ed's head. Improving the way cats do their business could be good business for him. So he packed five pounds of the odor-free, sponge-like clay in a paper bag, hoping to sell it to a pet store for sixty-five cents. The owner thought it was a crappy idea and doubted anyone would pay for the clay. So Ed said to just give away the product he had impulsively labeled "kitty litter."

Kitty Litter:

A creative thinker from Michigan has alleviated some of the mess in the lives of millions of cat owners.

Now for the rest of the scoop.... After years of pounding the pavement, selling the litter out of the back of his 1943 Chevy Coupe, Ed became a success, establishing himself as the founder of an industry that's grown so big it's now worth three-quarters of a billion dollars and even has its own lobbyist in Washington.

Fortunately for free-thinking Ed, he ignored the words cats fear to hear, "Don't you dare think about going outside the box."

A vendor skips up the aisles in the midst of a capacity crowd, hawking "hot dogs, popcorn, lugnuts!" And 11,000 zealous fans break out in song: "You got inhibitions, lose 'em, you got vocal chords, use 'em, you gotta go nuts, Lugnuts." What could be lunchtime at an auto plant is a normal break between innings at Oldsmobile Park.

The crowds are all devoted followers of the most unlikely baseball team in the history of the sport, the Lansing Lugnuts. The story began with owner Tom Dickson, an advertising exec so passionate about America's favorite pastime that he gave up his day job and purchased a minor-league team in Waterloo, Iowa, with a soon-to-be-condemned stadium (much to the chagrin of his wife, Sherry Myers, who wondered why he couldn't find another creative outlet, like taking piano lessons).

Before either could blink, they were headed to downtown Lansing with an obscure band of athletes in hopes of filling a new stadium's stands. More than 2,000 entries poured in for their name-the-team contest. On May 25, 1995, Lansing resident Jackie Borzich's "Lansing Lugnuts" was declared the winner, horrifying the town, which united in massive protests. Even David Letterman took to the airwaves, publicly ridiculing the LLs before his national audience.

But negative publicity can have positive side effects (just ask Martha Stewart). As it turns out, *Lansing Lugnuts* was a good thing and in 2004 was honored as the number-one sports name in a *USA Today* poll.

Nonstop entertainment keeps 400,000-patrons-a-year in the suites, seats, and picnic areas in side-splitting laughter. As part of the nuts-and-bolts routine, unsuspecting fans could be plucked to do the chicken dance or to sumo wrestle the Big Lug.

Tickets are available online at www.lansinglugnuts.com or by calling (517) 485–4800.

Lansing Lugnuts:

A minor league affiliate of the Toronto Blue Jays. Almost four million have watched the 'nuts become the pride of the state's capital.

Leelanau Sleeping Bear Dunes National Lakeshore is an area unto itself, encompassing a 34-mile stretch of lakes, river, beaches, and the impressive coastal sand dunes plus, North and South Manitou Islands. It is within this trio of geological miracles that our story takes place.

The Ojibway Indians are the true authors and are credited with naming Sleeping Bear Dunes after a bear-shaped, tree-covered bump that was eventually eroded by wind and water.

Legends are stories about life, evoking passion, empathy, and perhaps a few tears in both young and old. For as long as anyone can remember, this is the defining story of the National Lakeshore.

The Legend of the Sleeping Bear goes something like this: Long ago, in the land that is today Wisconsin, Mother Bear and her two cubs were driven into Lake Michigan by a raging forest fire. Although the cubs swam strongly, the distance and the water proved too much for them and they fell further and further behind, ultimately slipping beneath the waves. When Mother Bear reached the Michigan shore, she climbed to the top of a bluff and peered back across the water, searching in

Legend of the Sleeping Bear:

An Ojibway Indian tale of how the Sleeping Bear Sand Dunes were made.

vain for her cubs. The Great Spirit saw her and took pity on her plight. He raised North and South Manitou Islands to mark where her cubs vanished and laid a slumber upon Mother Bear.

Today the tale has become a book by Kathy-Jo Wargin; it was named official children's book of Michigan.

As sad as it may seem, the story offers hope for any mother who is separated from her children . . . and puts the onus on Wisconsin for instigating the dilemma in the first place.

you know you're in
michigan when...
...your license plate reads "IM N MI"

Life used to be so simple for Michigan State Troopers. Once upon a time there was a one-size-fits-all license plate with a clear-cut formula: two colors, three numbers, three letters, no Q's or O's, making a Michigander whirling down the freeway at 80 miles per hour easy to spot.

The years brought some monotony-busting, loyalty-building tweaking. Then came 1954, the year of the state slogan. After an exhaustive contest with more than 20,000 entries, the secretary of state narrowed it down to two: *Blue Waters* and *Water Wonderland,* the latter victorious and appearing on every plate for the next ten years.

The '54 single-style plates, for the first time, morphed into medium-blue with yellow letters, honoring the University of Michigan. The following year every vehicle sported green-and-white plates recognizing Michigan State University.

Momentum for diversity grew as ferocious as a true wolverine. At last count there were plates for twenty-four branches of military/veteran service, fifteen different universities, six special causes (water quality's the weakest seller), patriotic themes (pro-

ceeds going to the Salvation Army and Red Cross), and Olympic education, totaling forty-seven different license plate designs that Troopers today have to memorize.

Of course that isn't including the biggest state moneymakers: the personalized, or "I LUV ME" plates. More than 80,000 vanity plates have hit the highway since they were first issued in 1974 for an extra $30 annual service fee. Don't you wonder what possesses someone to fork over his hard-earned money to have his vehicle's backside plastered with a plate reading "I M BROK," "TOE BIZ," "EDUK8TR," or "LUV2BBQ"?

License Plates:

Customized plates make a vehicular fashion statement for drivers who want more "CARIZMA."

In addition to computers, cell phones, and some extra-strength Velcro, this two-piece state requires 42,000 miles of wire and 931,000 tons of concrete to keep its residents connected.

Poised over the Straits of Mackinac, the Mackinac Bridge—alias Big Mac or Mighty Mac—supplies the denture adhesive to the upper and lower peninsulas. Ferry boats first held the unifying job, carrying 10,351 vehicles during inaugural voyages in 1923. By 1950 demand grew so big that one weekend during deer-hunting season, more than 600,000 sets of wheels waited up to twelve hours for the ferries to sweep them to the other side.

The delays were permanently eliminated with the Big Mac's opening on November 1, 1957. Standing 5 miles long and tall enough for Great Lakes freighters to pass comfortably underneath, it's the largest suspension bridge in the western hemisphere.

You're allowed to put your feet on the bridge just one day out of the year. The 7:00 A.M. Labor Day Mackinac Bridge Walk has become a favorite pedestrian tradition, attracting more than 60,000 who can then say they've walked with the governor, the official leader of the pack.

The folks who operate Michigan's famous elevated crossing understand that some

Mackinac Bridge:

The publicly-held Mackinac Bridge is the only stretch of concrete exclusively within the state's borders to charge a toll.

drivers suffer from *gephyrophobia*—a fear of bridges. Special complimentary assistance is available for drivers not comfortable enough to keep their eyes open while crossing the span.

When you're in Mackinaw City, stop by Stilwell's Mama Mia Pizzeria at 231 East Central Street (231–436–5534). The second floor houses the Mackinac Bridge Museum, filled with eclectic memorabilia of the 3,500 who worked for three years on the project that's keeping Michigan together.

Info on all bridge services and fares can be accessed at www.mackinacbridge.org.

you know you're in
michigan when...
... you travel Somewhere in Time

Probably the closest you can ever come to time travel is on Mackinac Island, an island in the U.P. where you can escape life as you know it today. Cars and trucks are banned, and pooper-scooping is a full-time occupation.

Air is cleaner here. In fact, everything is cleaner here except for occasional streets (horse diapers are forbidden, to prevent chafed rears). So pristine and picturesque is this state park, *Conde Nast Traveler* magazine named it one of the top twenty islands in the world.

Remnants of the Revolutionary War remain alive at Fort Mackinac, built by British soldiers. (Warning: The hourly cannon-firing demonstrations can knock people off their rockers on the famous porch at the Grand Hotel.)

Its Edwardian romance caught the eye of Hollywood, which made the cult classic *Somewhere in Time,* starring Jane Seymour and Christopher Reeve, here. The film is more popular today than during its 1980 release. Each October thousands of movie devotees swarm the island to play out every scene again and again.

Most of the island shuts down for the winter, when the ferry boats are frozen out of business. Small planes and snowmobiles shuttle the 500 year-round residents back and forth to the mainland for routine business like barbers, dentists, and buying feed for the horses.

Mackinac Island:

Bicycles are the transportation of choice in the summer. In winter a row of trees lining the lake's ice tells snowmobilers where it's safe to drive.

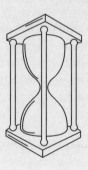

you know you're in
michigan when...
... you've got a magical Colon

Wave a magic wand over a town of 1,200 and with a quick blink of the eye, it more than doubles its population for one week every August. No surprise here since Colon, Michigan, is the magic capital of the world. Here you'll see giant black top-hat planters lining its downtown, and the high school has bragging rights to the only fighting rabbit as a mascot.

Magician Harry Blackstone Sr. put Colon on the magic map when he purchased hundreds of acres of land here in the 1920s, ultimately becoming a Pied Piper for other conjurers.

It's proved to be fertile ground for abracadabra paraphernalia, too. Abbott's Magic Company—now known as the Neiman Marcus of its field—pulled open its curtains in 1934 to unveil thousands of sleight-of-hand tricks to the trade. That same year Abbott's began its famous "Magic Get Together," a weeklong hocus-pocus party drawing magicians from every corner of the globe. Housing them all may be the biggest feat. Hotels are nonexistent here, forcing a fleet of RVs and motor homes to appear out of thin air.

The whole town lives, breathes, and dies magic. Nearby Lakeside Cemetery is the final resting place for numerous stage performers including three generations of Blackstones and Karrel "Milky the Clown"

Magical Colon:

Dissected by the colon-shaped St. Joseph River, hocus pocus is a daily occurrence in this town.

Fox, whose three-word epitaph says it all: "It was fun."

In the mid-1800s, postmaster Lorensie Schellhouse sought advice from above when it came to putting a name on the map. Totally stumped, he haphazardly opened a dictionary, pointed his finger on the page, and there it was...*colon*. Fodder for continuous jokes, Greg Border, owner of Abbott's, claims he lives just outside the city limits, making him a "semi-colon."

Learn the pro's secrets at Abbott's at 124 St. Joseph Street, (800) 92–MAGIC.

you know you're in
michigan when...
...u-turn, right, and you've made a Michigan left

Proceed with caution when someone gives you directions that include making a "Michigan left." That's because you'll be making a legal U-turn, followed by a right turn in order to avoid making an illegal left turn.

Confusing? You bet. Out-of-towners or those new to Michigan scratch their heads when introduced to the concept.

Yet, with a little background, this form of traffic control makes perfect sense.

A Michigan left can be made only at an intersection where at least one road is a divided highway. When a left turn is forbidden, you must drive approximately 660 feet past the street on which you want to turn left. At that point you'll find a U-turn lane. When traffic is clear, you complete your "U," quickly getting over to the right-hand side at the intersection, where you'll turn right, putting you where you would have gone if left turns had been allowed.

Michigan lefts were created in 1960 by the Michigan Highway Department to eliminate the backup caused by making turns at divided highways. Telegraph and 8 Mile Road in Detroit were the first to see the confounding turns. Deemed a success with improved traffic movement, their continued

Michigan Left:

A polite, hopefully expeditious, and unique method of turning left through a series of left and right turns.

expansion has grown more than 700 intersections in the state, including many in the Upper Peninsula.

While Michigan officials are proud of their innovation, no other state in the country has turned on to their turn, leaving Michigan standing alone in the crossroads of traffic.

you know you're in
michigan when...
...a television show has its own museum

Good thing Ted Turner started CNN before Barry Stutesman and Dell Vaughan came on the scene. Rose City's self-proclaimed country boys are going gangbusters doing what they love: directing, producing, and starring in their own weekly TV show.

Michigan Magazine is a half-hour of down-home fun, focusing on "everything and any-thing Michigan, as long as it's positive." One week a woman from Chesaning could be sharing her secrets for forming a local chapter of the Red Hat Society. The next week it might be someone like Traverse City-area's John Shepherd, who, in his quest for UFOs, renovated his entire home to broadcast music "straight up into the heavens" twenty-four hours a day.

Their TV menu also has the standard bill of fare: potters, artists, musicians, and all the other Michiganians who otherwise wouldn't get their fifteen minutes of fame.

With their show broadcast on public televi-sion stations throughout the state, Stutesman and Vaughan have now taken the program nationwide to RFD, rural America's number-one network.

But their talents don't stop there. Since the show's 1990 inception, their product line has grown to include a magazine, cook-books, music CDs (Vaughan wrote the show's theme song, "Soar Like an Eagle"), and sweatshirts.

Because everyone who has appeared on the show has given them something, in 1998 Stutesman and Vaughan opened their own *Michigan Magazine* Museum. All 5,000 square feet are "right full" of hats, guitars, grandfather clocks, a handwritten note from the composer of Elvis's hit "Heartbreak Hotel," and a 3,500-pound Indian head from an Onaway metalworker.

Eventually the duo's 1994 Silhouette, do-nated by Oldsmobile, will go into the mu-seum as well. In the meantime it'll continue to transport them all around Michigan, while the odometer rolls well past 500,000 miles.

The museum, on Highway 33 between Fairview and Cummings, is open mid-June through Labor Day. For hours call (989) 848–2246. *Michigan Magazine* TV show also has its own Web site: www.michigan magazine.com. Or you can contact Barry and Dell personally at (989) 685–2634.

Michigan Magazine:

Two Rose City "country boys" have become media moguls, putting more than 500,000 miles on their Oldsmobile as they scout out the state.

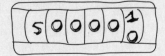

55

you know you're in
michigan when...
...you know it like the back of your hand

There isn't a single person in the state of Michigan who hasn't used his hands to indicate where he lives. Some people have said that this alone would prevent them from living anywhere else.

No one knows for certain how the practice of mapping on our hands got started. Some say the guys in the late 1700s who drew up the state lines apparently wanted to put a map in the hands of every family. What's the cheapest way to do it? Create a state that looks just like the perfectly shaped outline of your hand so no one ever has an excuse for getting lost.

Putting the map together does require the use of both hands and some coordination. First, take your right hand, palm facing up, fingers pointing away from you. That's what you use as the Lower Peninsula.

Then rest your left hand, again palm facing up, on top of your right fingertips with your left fingers pointing right. Make sure you line up the middle finger of your right hand with the last joint on your pinkie. Pull your left thumb in so that it sits at a 45-degree angle to your index finger. Now you have the Upper Peninsula.

And you're ready to point away to your heart's content. Mount Pleasant sits smack dab in the middle of your right palm, while Northport is on the top of your (right) pinkie. Ask anyone in Marlette, Cass City, or Port Austin and they'll tell you they're proud to live in the (right) thumb, while residents in Cheboygan are among the legitimate few who can use their (right) middle finger to signal their home.

The U.P. works the same, although it helps if you have an arthritic bump or a large wart to signal southern cities like Menominee. Houghton is easy—it's the first joint of your left thumb.

Depending on how many creases you have on your hands, you could be lucky enough to indicate major thoroughfares, too.

The whole premise is a godsend for the man who refuses to ask for directions.

Michigan Map:

Born with a map of Michigan on their hand, everyone uses it to point to the finger, knuckle, or palm area where they live.

you know you're in
michigan when...

...you're in a perpetual state of confusion

People who reside full-time in Michigan, or those known as "snowbirds" who temporarily migrate south in the winter, have been fighting an identity crisis all their lives. We've become a modern version of *Three Faces of Eve*. Do we refer to ourselves as Michiganders, Michiganites, or Michiganians?

The choice is really up to you. *Michigander* makes you sound like something fowl. Choose *Michiganite* and you could be mistaken for a mineral. *Michiganian* was coined in the 1870s edition of *The Collections of the Michigan Pioneer and Historical Society,* a group not known for their shenanigans.

Legislators have tried for years to come to a consensus on an "official" title, but in typical government fashion, after all the bickering, nothing has been settled.

The two largest newspapers in the state can't even agree. The *Detroit Free Press* uses "-gander" while the *Detroit News* prefers "-ganian."

One theory is that the longer you've lived here, the more likely you are to use *Michigander*. Shorter stays are *Michiganians*.

This whole debate could be blamed on Abraham Lincoln, who in 1848 was running for president against Lewis Cass, first gov-

Michigander, Michiganian, or Michiganite:

State legislators have eternally struggled with the proper name for their constituents.

ernor of the Michigan territory. Cass was perceived by Abe as a fool, an idiot, or, in his words, a goose from Michigan; out of which was derived *Michigander*. Hardly a term of endearment.

Why would anyone want to be compared to a silly goose? But it seems they do. Surveys have found that most people go with *Michigander*, as do most spell-checkers. (*Michiganian* is a no-no to the computer.) Maybe because in our frenzied society, it's easier to have one less syllable in the word, using less time to speak

Either way, it looks like we're in a perpetual gridlock. But then, what's good for the Michigoose is good for the Michigander.

you know you're in
michigan when...
...roads are like family, ever-present and quirky

Michigan drivers may be the most color-blind lot in the nation. When approaching an amber light, they put the pedal to the metal. Since when did the *a* in amber stand for "accelerate?" Maybe as long ago as 1920, when the nation's first four-way traffic signal was installed at the Detroit intersection of Woodward and Fort Streets. Or perhaps it was 1937, when Michigan took the lead in publishing the first how-to manual for drivers.

Either way, the state has been a magnet for traffic-law breakers since 1909, when the country's first $13,534.59-mile of concrete pavement was laid on Woodward between Six and Seven Mile Roads.

Here are some tips on how to survive Michigan on the road....

Like most places, east/west interstates are even-numbered, and north/south are odd-numbered—unless you're on Interstate 69 east of Lansing, when for more than a hundred miles it becomes an eastern beeline to Michigan's thumb.

Interstates are always addressed by their formal titles. It's "I–75" and "I–94." Never refer to them as "75" or "94" like you would your last-name-only buddy. Occasionally they do have a more personal name. Branching out from Detroit through its northern city limits, I–75 becomes "The

Michigan Roads:

Beware, after a rough winter, the state's concrete lanes are filled with more potholes than motorists.

Chrysler," and in the opposite direction it's "The Fisher," sharing the surname of "Freeway."

Identity crises have struck many thoroughfares. Troy's Big Beaver becomes Quarton to the west and Metro Parkway to the east, when it's really all Sixteen Mile Road. Same goes for M–59, a.k.a. Huron or Hall Road.

Wherever the road takes you, you need to watch what you say: Schoenherr is "SHAY-ner"; Dequindre is "Duh-KWIN-der"; Lahser is "LAAH-sir" (rhyming with "ah, sir"); and Gratiot, named for 1812 war veteran General Charles Gratiot, is properly pronounced "GRASH-it," as in "crash it."

you know you're in
michigan when...
... O'Geeze and O'Pete aren't from Ireland

When newcomers take their first steps on Michigan soil, they're glutted with a welcome basket of guidebooks, road maps, water navigational charts, and discount coupons to the nearest dollar store, when what they really need is a simple glossary of the local language.

Yes, English, or a Canadian derivative of it, is spoken throughout the state. But it's how we use it that causes those head-scratching moments. Here are some examples:

- **Yooper:** Someone residing in the Upper Peninsula (see page 100).

- **Troll:** A term used to describe anyone living under "The Bridge"—always implying the Mackinac Bridge—separating them from Yoopers living above.

- **Up North:** Two words indicating the line of demarcation as anything north of Lansing. On weekends, everyone heads "up north" (all relative, depending on your starting point) to relax in their "cottage" (anything from a multimillion-dollar lakefront log home to a one-room shed with a porta-potty out back).

- **O'Geeze:** A catch-all phrase used to simplify an infinite collection of exclamatory explanations, i.e.: "That's a beaut," "Ain't that somethin'," "How disgusting," or "What a shame."

- **Geeze O'Pete:** First cousin to the aforementioned, with an added exclamation point. A polite alternative to four-letter words when your teenager drives through the garage door.

- **Ren Cen:** Sounds like a breath mint, looks like five towers standing guard over the Detroit River; a preferred nickname for the Renaissance Center. One of the largest privately funded real estate projects in history, the hotel/office/shopping complex also represents one of the all-time worst investments. The Ren Cen, the brainchild of Henry Ford II (a.k.a. "The Deuce"), opened in 1977 to the tune of $250 million, and nineteen years later it was gobbled up by General Motors for a measly $73 million, precipitating a statewide chorus of "Geeze O'Pete."

Michigan-speak:

Local phrases take on new meaning in this combination of Yoopanese and Troll talk.

you know you're in
michigan when...
...Motown means mo' music

In the late 1950s Michigan's automotive industry took a back seat to "The Sound of Young America." It happened in a modest Detroit home so small that someone had to stand guard to make sure the toilets weren't flushed during recording sessions. The new music of the youth of America, an incomparable mixture of rhythm 'n' blues and soul, transformed itself into the Motortown Revue, eventually shortened to the universally recognized name of Motown.

Berry Gordy Jr., an $85-a-week Lincoln-Mercury assembly-line worker, was the man behind the music, a visionary entrepreneur who borrowed $800 to create America's fourth-largest record company. As a producer, his first hit was Barrett Strong's "Money (That's What I Want)" in 1959. Just two years later Gordy got the money he wanted with his first million-dollar-seller—"Shop Around" by the Miracles.

Motown Records was able to capitalize on the growing passion with car radios, creating shorter songs and setting up car speakers in their studio so engineers would know just what "Baby Love" would sound like to a motorist's ear.

Gordy used to say there was something special about Michigan and its wealth of local musical talent. The world didn't disagree, granting superstar status to names like Smokey Robinson and the Miracles, Diana Ross and the Supremes, Marvin Gaye, Stevie Wonder, and The Temptations. Never forgetting his roots, Gordy made sure all of his artists' publicity shots included an auto, usually a prestigious Cadillac.

Some say the music world's most famous melody consists of just twelve notes—the classic solo guitar lick at the very beginning of "My Girl." The infectious rhythm was the brainchild of one of the Funk Brothers, a group of fourteen musicians who were the anonymous heart and soul of Motown. Together they played on more number-one records than the Beatles, the Beach Boys, the Rolling Stones, and Elvis Presley combined, yet not one person outside the industry ever knew their name.

Motown Music:

A beat with heart and soul from the town that got people up and dancing in the streets.

you know you're in
michigan when...
... muskrat's on the menu

Long lines form early on the day tickets to this highly coveted culinary experience go on sale. Yes, people are hoping not to be left out of the opportunity to savor the wintertime delicacy known as muskrat. Each January and February dozens of VFW halls, churches, and private clubs in Monroe host bountiful banquets with the furry rodent (the fur is gone; a few small bones remain) as the main entree.

Peak hunting season is December through mid-March, since the marsh rabbit, as it's known in the area, is in heat the other nine months of the year. Muskrat meals, steeped in 200 years of tradition, began when hungry French settlers requested and received special dispensation from the church to allow consumption of the meat on Fridays.

Others pondered the creature's true identity. It lives in the water, so it's not an animal. It walks on land, therefore not a fish. Their verdict? A vegetable.

Whatever the vegetarian muskrat is, loyal fans can't get enough of it, especially when the rich—so dark, it's almost black—meat is parboiled with wine and onions and topped with creamed-corn gravy, a preparation to whet the appetite of the biggest skeptic.

Muskrat:

In Monroe it's considered a mouth-watering delicacy, served with a flavorful sauce. Is that the strains of Captain and Tennille's "Muskrat Love" playing softly in the background?

Monroe rightly calls itself "Muskrat Town of the World," evidenced by the 4-foot-high statues scattered around the streets, all dedicated to their beloved 'rat.

If you can't get in to one of the club dinners, Kola's Food Factory at 17168 Fort Street in Riverview (734–281–0477) offers year-round dine-in or home delivery of muskrat with garlic mashed potatoes. Or check with the Monroe County Historical Museum (734–281–0477) for the latest public tastings.

you know you're in
michigan when...
...you pass through Alaska, Delaware, and Wyoming

How cities get their names would make for a stimulating doctoral thesis, or at least decorous toilet paper trivia. Michigan could supply more that its fair share of fodder.

Take mundane *Michigan Center.* Credit goes to a master of the obvious.

Give a point to *Alaska, Delaware, Dublin, Phoenix, St. Louis, Vermontville,* and *Wyoming* for placing one foot outside their comfort zone.

There are cities of aspiration like *Hope, Liberty,* and *Fortune Lake.* Feel-good places like *Bliss, Kind(e), Paradise, Nirvana,* and *Bath. Witch Lake* and *Hell* would be good twin cities, even though they're on different peninsulas. Same goes for *Christmas* and *Holly.*

Pines Stump Junction, Alamo, and *Frontier* don't sound like they belong in the Midwest. Neither do *Aloha* or *Mikado.* But they're here.

Don't you wonder if there are really any rose bushes in *Rosebush,* pigeons in *Pigeon,* or wooden shoes in *Wooden Shoe?* How much oil is there in *Oil City?* Do people even know how to waltz in *Waltz?* Why would anyone want to move to a place named *Rust? Alabaster* and *Argyle* sound more attractive. *Two Heart* is better than one *Palms.*

Someone should give a prize for the city that best exemplifies creative word play. Hands down that award would go to *Bad Axe* and its football team, the Bad Axe Hatchets.

Finally, what better way to culminate this frivolous list than with a rural town discovered by Daniel B. Eldred, who, in 1835, decided to end his search for a perfect place to live in *Climax, Michigan.*

Names:

Novi, named for railway stop No. VI, is one of many Michigan cities with peculiar naming histories.

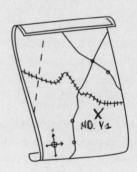

you know you're in
michigan when...
...fame is almost all downhill

Here's good practice for a *Jeopardy* contestant:

Answer: The birthplace of organized skiing in America.

Question: What is Ishpeming, Michigan?

The birth was a natural for the town where snow has been known to fall at the rate of two feet a day as early as October.

The Ishpeming Ski Club, founded in 1887 and one of the oldest continually active ski clubs in the country, had a glimmer in its eye when, in the winter of 1904–1905 it became the single parent of the National Ski Association (now politically corrected to National Ski and Snowboard Association).

Since 1954 the organization has operated the U.S. National Ski Hall of Fame and Museum, offering 14,000 visitors a year from all fifty states and more than thirty-five foreign countries the opportunity to relive skiing history while staying toasty-warm.

The museum's newest $1.7-million home is a two-story sleek, contemporary structure with roof lines resembling ski jumps. Inside are more than one hundred exhibits, including a collection of vintage ski lifts; a magnificent mural depicting the work of the American Tenth Mountain Division during World War II; a 1,300-volume ski library; and a theater.

National Ski Hall of Fame:

A museum in the heart of snow country dedicated to the ups and downs of ski heroes everywhere.

The U.S. National Ski Hall of Fame and Museum is located at 61 Palms Avenue in Ishpeming. For more information call (906) 485–6323 or log on to www.skihall.com.

Contrary to popular opinion, not everyone in the Hall of Fame went downhill. Of the 342 inductees (as of 2005), there are those who traveled cross-country to get where they are today.

you know you're in
michigan when...
...everything's official, even the state dirt

States are notorious for designating official this 'n' that, and Michigan is no exception. Receiving an official designation is no easy task, requiring a Representative or Senate sponsor; going through first, second, third readings; going in and out of committee; and so on and so forth. Basically it's the same process as getting any other bill passed.

Michigan's Great Seal was the first of the "officials," in 1835. Next came the apple blossom as the official state flower, followed by the state flag, and, in 1931, the robin as state bird, a decision coming under fire lately. Two bills are pending to rid the robin of his perch, naming the new state bird as either Kirtland's warbler or the black-capped chickadee. It's hard to imagine that decisions on health-care funding and balancing the budget have become more important to some lawmakers.

Other state designations include:
Song: "My Michigan" (1937)
Tree: White pine (1955)
Stone: Petoskey stone (1965)
Gem: Isle Royale greenstone (1973)
Fish: Brook trout (1988)
Soil: Kalkaska dirt (1990)
Reptile: Painted turtle (1995)
Game mammal: Whitetailed deer (1997)
Wildflower: Dwarf lake iris (1998)
Fossil: Mastodon (2002)
Historical Society: Historical Society of

"Officials":

Michigan has an "official" everything, even an "official" list of pending "official" hopefuls.

Michigan (2002; you were expecting the Purple Hat Society?)

Then there's the list of wannabes, all "officially" sponsored bills that have not yet been confirmed:
State waltz: Wolverine Waltz
State plant: Soybean
State insect: Green darner dragonfly
State agriculture insect: Honeybee
State burger: Cherry burger (a concoction of Traverse City's Pleva Market)
State dog: Golden retriever (owners of yorkies, poodles, and spaniels will surely unite against this one)

you know you're in
michigan when...
...Olympians roam the halls

Next time you're near Northern Michigan University (NMU) in Marquette, take a closer look at the gold and silver necklaces students are wearing. They may not be as they first appear. Here is one place where you could be in the same classroom with an Olympic gold medal winner in boxing, luge, speed-skating, cross-country, and biathlon. (As of 2004, add women's wrestling to that list, too.)

NMU is America's only college displaying the Olympic rings. Designated in 1985 as the sole Olympic Education Training Center, NMU is a place where athletes train brain and body. Speed skating's gold and silver medalist Cathy Turner and gold medal boxing champ David Reid are both graduates of the program.

If the master plan succeeds, Marquette will be the site of a future Winter Olympics. The components are all in place: the snow, cold, educated athletes, and the world's largest wooden sports dome, covering 5.1 acres under one roof. The Superior Dome, with its multi-purpose retractable turf, is fifteen stories high with a diameter of 536 feet. It has seating for 8,000, enough to accommodate the combined populations of several U.P. cities.

Apparently ice has various speeds because Peif Athletic Complex is said to have the fastest sheets anywhere, setting six world speed-skating records on its surface.

Just one ingredient is missing from the Olympic formula: a vertical drop to comply with alpine skiing standards. Most Olympic cites have drops in the thousands. Michigan's biggest is Mt. Bohemia, north of Houghton, at 900 feet.

Olympic Education Training Center:

Marquette's strategy is to some day host the Olympics—if you train the athletes, the games will come.

A good day in Michigan is any day the sun shines. A bad day is when a Michigander has to step on a scale.

There's a good reason hospital gurneys are stronger, church pews are built with more support, and seats in movie theaters have expanded from 19 to 23 inches. The state's population is growing by pounds and inches, ranked as one of the most overweight in the country. At last tally, two-thirds of residents were considered to be feasting and tasting in excess. For years, Detroit was the plumpest U.S. city, dropping to second place behind Houston in 2004.

We are creatures of bad habits: 17 percent binge-drink; 25 percent smoke; and 75 percent don't get the daily requirements of thirteen fruits and vegetables a day accompanied by ninety minutes of daily exercise (although it does seem like all that walking back and forth to the refrigerator should count for something).

Our expanding girths just don't add up sensibly. Michigan has a plethora of hiking and biking trails, lakes for swimming and water-skiing, and snow for skiing and snowmobiling. And if you don't like one of those, there's always bowling. One hour of bowling burns 259 calories on the frame of a

Overweight:

If a resident's worth was measured by his or her girth, Michigan would be the richest (instead of the heftiest) state in the nation.

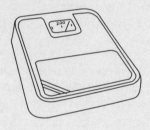

190-pound person. Greater Detroit has long been considered the bowling capital of the world.

On the other hand Michigan is weighted down with pizza. Home to ten separate franchise headquarters, including Little Caesar's and Domino's, Michigan has always been known for being loyal to its own. Just another reason why Michigan also has America's largest Weight Watchers franchise.

you know you're in
michigan when...
...Fat Tuesday turns into paczki-mania

One word has done more than any other to keep Michigan waistlines expanding: *paczki*. For the uninitiated, it's a deep-fried dough ball, most often filled with custard or with strawberry, lemon, or prune jam, all adding up to a whopping 450 calories; more than one Whopper sandwich. Overindulging in paczki has become a day-before-Ash-Wednesday, or Fat Tuesday, tradition.

Paczki consumption began in Poland as one gluttonous blowout in preparation for the fasting period of Lent. Heck, everyone's Polish on Fat Tuesday.

You need some practice to say the word correctly. (That should burn up a few calories right there.) It's pronounced "POONCH key" or "PUNCH key." Either way, the accent goes on the first syllable. The singular form is *paczek* and is spoken as "PON check." But just as an old potato chip commercial said, "Betcha can't eat just one." Nobody does, so the singular form becomes irrelevant.

On Fat Tuesday the mouthwatering gooey orbs inspire people to set their alarms early, or not go to bed at all, so they can be first in line when the bakeries open, somewhere between 3:00 and 5:00 A.M.

The North American birthplace of the paczki is Hamtramck, so it's only natural the city pulls out all the stops, sponsoring paczki-eating contests (a fourteen-year-old consumed ten and a half in fifteen minutes), selling paczki bobble heads, and putting on the Paczki Parade.

As they waddle their way down the parade route, Poles and honorary Poles alike belt out the musical group The Polish Muslims' rendition of "Ode to the Paczki," sung to the Beatles' tune "Yesterday."

"Paczki Day
All the tourists come Hamtramck's way
And I add ten pounds to what I weigh
Oh, I believe in Paczki Day."

Paczki:

A deep-fried dough ball, filled with jelly or custard, providing a month's worth of fat calories and carbohydrates.

you know you're in
michigan when...
...Paradise and Hell are just a peninsula apart

How lucky can one state get? Hell and Paradise coexisting happily in Michigan. And for years an eerie sort of attraction has been pulling them together.

Fittingly, Hell sits in the Lower Peninsula, far below Paradise, which is elevated in the uppermost peak of the eastern section of the Upper Peninsula.

Hell is the older of the two, discovered in 1841. Obviously it took a little more work to reach Paradise, established in 1925.

More people live in Paradise: 2,508. Just shy of 200 fluctuate through the cinder city.

Paradise is a nature-lover's Heaven on Earth. Pristine forests filled with lush vegetation provide perfect trails to walk in the summer and ecstasy for snowmobilers in the winter. The streets of Hell are dotted with only three stores.

Call it uncanny, but when the Great Fire of 1922 decimated the land of Paradise, it left fertile ground for wild blueberries. Residents may have trouble remembering their mother's maiden name, but just ask them about blueberry-picking spots and the answer rolls instantly off the tips of their tongues.

Paradise is quite capable of showing its devilish side, raising some Hell each Halloween with its Haunted Trail, 400 yards of "terror, fun, and visually cool effects."

Most curious is the result of a study conducted by a local Boy Scout troop seeking to find the precise difference between Paradise and Hell. A round trip between the two cities was recorded to be a diabolically unnerving 666 miles.

Paradise and Hell:

Two small-town cities a peninsula apart, each striving to make a unique name for itself.

you know you're in
michigan when...
...pasties are something you eat

Pasty—It's a funny word. *Webster*'s classifies it as a noun and, depending on how you pronounce it, the meaning changes dramatically.

When you say it "PAHS-tee" with a short a, as in the word *past,* it refers to a meat pie that sticks to your ribs, the meal of choice for people in the Upper Peninsula for years. If you choose to voice it as "PAYS-tee" with a long a, you're talking about something else adhering to your body, a little higher than the ribs, that's evolved into the mainstay for dancers in Las Vegas. Many a local newscaster has turned beet-red after realizing his or her mispronunciation.

The Upper Peninsula has had a love affair with the pasty ("PAHS-tee") since the days of copper mining. While in the shaft, miners would heat their pasty—a meat-potato-carrot-onion meal in a crust—with the heat from the candles on their hats.

Although the mines are no longer in operation, the quirky meat pie is alive and well. In fact, the residents of Still Waters Community Elders Home in Calumet, a seventy-bed assisted living facility, have turned the foodstuff into a nationally recognized business. It all began when many of the home's residents, who had been miners, requested the labor-intensive food item be added to the weekly menu, offering to help chop carrots or peel potatoes to make it.

Pasties:

A U.P. version of the calzone, where meat, potatoes, and carrots all come together under one shell.

Word of their culinary talents spread quickly and in 1995, thanks to the Internet and the home's administrator, Charlie Hopper, a mail-order business began. Now each Monday and Tuesday, their USDA-approved kitchen ships the country's only 100 percent handmade pasties to hungry consumers in all fifty states.

In addition to receiving many awards for their ingenious Web site, www.pasty.com, one of their proudest tributes is the photo of California's governor, Arnold Schwarzenegger. The governator is biting into a Still Waters pasty as he makes good on a friendly wager when the Los Angeles Lakers lost the 2004 NBA championship to the Detroit Pistons.

you know you're in
michigan when...
...the Stone Age never left Petoskey

Geology aficionados take note. Michigan didn't have a state fossil until 2002 (*mammut americanum,* or mastodon), but for forty years it had a fossil—the *hexagonaria percarinata*—for its state stone, making it the first state ever to designate a fossil as an official state symbol.

In lay terms, Michigan's designated stone, the Petoskey, is fossilized coral, a remnant of the Devonian Period 350 million years ago, when we were close to the equator luxuriating in our own prehistoric hot tub.

A six-sided irregular honeycomb pattern in shades of grayish brown makes the smooth Petoskey stone easy to identify as you stroll along northern Michigan beaches. Rougher versions, which haven't been through the bump-and-grind tumble cycle, are generally found inland.

Most Petoskey stones are about the size of a potato. In 1999, however, one Leelanau resident stumbled upon the biggest Petoskey to date—weighing one ton, measuring 40 inches by 20 inches—while trolling for a nice jewelry stone in the Sleeping Bear Sand Dunes.

Ottawa Indian traders are believed to have been the first to recognize the fossils centuries ago. Legend has it that Petoskey was named for a wealthy fur trader, the son of a local French Indian chief (you read that cor-

Petoskey Stone:

The state's official stone is a freckled-faced, rough-around-the-edges fossil, coveted for all forms of jewelry.

rectly), who at his birth was surrounded by glorious sunshine, or *petosegay,* meaning "rising sun" or "sunbeams of promise."

The best time to go stone-hunting is early spring, after the ice has melted and a new crop is pushed to shore. Ironically, experts say the best place to find a Petoskey stone isn't in Petoskey, but rather in neighboring Charlevoix, specifically at the south end of the beach in what's known as Petoskey State Park.

Anyone really in-the-know will also tell you to head to the nearest gift shop where you can purchase one, already pre-polished, for about $4.00.

Don't be surprised if you read in one of Michigan's small town obituaries, "Going hunting just won't be the same without Grandma's pickled eggs." Where else, but in the resourceful hands of home cooks, would you be able to take two dozen left-over Easter eggs and turn them into palatable provisions for campers?

The name *pickled eggs* may be hard to swallow, but there are those who are true-blue to the gastronomic anomaly. Basically, these dubious delicacies are canned hard-boiled eggs, easy to transport, with a shelf life that'll outlast many a movie star's next marriage.

Start with the core ingredients, vinegar and eggs, sprinkle with sugar, and put the mixture into hibernation. A few eye-popping additives will give them an extra kick. Mix some beets in the blend and you'll have pleasantly plump purple pickled eggs right through to their lavender-colored yolk, while jalapeño pickled eggs are sure to heat up the coldest winter night.

Some colleges have TGIF parties; Michigan Tech in Houghton has pickled egg-making parties, probably not a good idea for a first date.

Of course, if all this sounds like way too much work but your taste buds are still tempted, head over to one of the many Jerky Outlets in mid-Michigan, where you can buy a jar of hot or mild pickled eggs, smoked eggs, or the always irresistible turkey gizzards.

On second thought, maybe it would just be easier to fill the chickens' water dishes with vinegar and have them lay the eggs already pickled.

Pickled Eggs:

These pickled sweet 'n' sour canned eggs have been a perennial favorite of hunters.

you know you're in
michigan when...
...pop is a beverage

It's become somewhat of a linguistics Civil War. When referring to a carbonated soft drink, should you call it "pop" or "soda?" Just remember that in Michigan we say "pop," and to avoid becoming ostracized from society, never ask for "soda" here. Don't try to combine the two either. "Soda pop" just doesn't cut it here. We can become real soda jerks when it comes to our pop.

Let's take a closer look at why we're right in calling it "pop" and why the rest of the country should follow our lead.

First, the word *pop* refers to the bottle used to package the beverage; hence the term *pop bottle*. Ben and Perry Feigenson, founders of Faygo in Detroit, started calling their drink "pop" in 1910 because when they opened the bottle the sound went "pop." When someone on the East Coast opens his or her bottle, does it go "soda?"

Second, a soda has ice cream in it; any dictionary will substantiate that. Does it make any sense to call a Diet Coke a soda?

The pop-versus-soda controversy has inflamed such regional passions that an entire Web site is devoted to it. The site www.popvssoda.com began as a college research project and continuously does online questioning to see who's right.

Pop:

A logical local reference for any flavored, carbonated beverage, soft drink, or POP: Pool of Phosphorus.

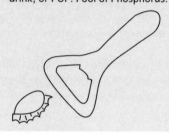

Their state-by-state study found that Michigan leads the nation in the number of respondents who use "pop" as the term of choice. "Pop" leads "soda" nationally, too, albeit by a slim margin, 39.31 percent to 37.54 percent. (The "other" category brings the total to 100 percent.)

In the words of the study's directors, however, none of whom are from Michigan, "People who say 'pop' are much, much cooler." Case closed.

you know you're in
michigan when...
... sailors hit high C

You can tell a lot about an event by its sponsor, and the Bacardi Bayview Mackinac Race is certainly no exception. Yo, ho, ho with a bottle of rum in hand, the race captains shout out "Party Hearty!" as thousands on Port Huron's Black River unleash their inhibitions with free-spirited capers to rival the wildest fraternity party.

The days leading up to the start of the world's largest fresh-water sporting event are as fun-filled for spectators as they are for the occasionally tipsy landlocked sailors. Detroit's Bayview Yacht Club is the mastermind behind the prestigious seafaring tradition, going on since 1925 and formerly known as the Port Huron-to-Mackinac Island Sailboat Race. Each July more than 265 boats, ranging in size from 26 to 90 feet, sail north on Lake Huron aiming to be the first to cross the finish line some 250 miles away.

The famous and not-so-famous alike all have faced less-than-smooth sailing conditions. Picture Walt Disney, Ted Turner, Bob Seger, or Gordon Lightfoot at the helm battling winds of up to 45 miles per hour with 9-foot waves.

They've all been through the thrill of spending hours at sea—ninety-two hours, forty-one minutes was the longest—and lived to share their "sail tales," increasingly exaggerated with each retelling. Successful completion of twenty-five years of navigating the course qualifies one for membership in the "Society of Mackinac Billy Goats" (amended in 1984 to include nanny goats— U. S. Representative Candace Miller is one).

Anyone can watch the colorful Saturday morning start from Port Huron's Lakeside Park, provided you're awake by 11:30 A.M. Mackinac Island's where it all wraps up, late Sunday and Monday.

Port Huron-to-Mackinac Race:

A sailor's dream is to go Bridge-to-Bridge (Bluewater to Mackinac) in the shortest amount of time.

you know you're in
michigan when...
...your chips are home-grown

Michigan and Silicon Valley share the same claim as top producers of high-demand chip material, though Michigan's business model presents itself as more well-grounded. Farmers engineer the state's $100-million potato crop to fill up nearly every single potato chip bag in the country.

There's something about our home-grown spuds that people crave, especially locals who each consume seven pounds of potato chips a year, almost double the national per-person average of four pounds. No wonder Michigan is touted as America's Potato Chip Capital.

While many of the tubers are shipped out of state, a number stay in Detroit to make the seven-minute conversion from raw potato to a handful of chips. Better Made opened its manufacturing doors on April 1, 1930; Uncle Ray's started in 1965. Both have remained successful with an ever-expanding line of flavors, though barbecue remains the area's fave.

Uncle Ray, really Ray Jenkins, may someday become the Baskin-Robbins of potato chips. Currently he's got fifteen don't-knock-'em-till-you've-tried-'em flavors like kosher dill, ketchup, mustard, onion, roasted garlic, and the all-inclusive coney.

Jenkins himself is somewhat of a chip-off-the-old-block. A few years back he began writing his autobiography, opting to publish it on his snack bags. Included on every package are various tales about his life, whether in the eighth grade or at his first job at the Great Lakes Grey Iron Foundry, followed by inspirational Biblical quotes.

To continue pleasurable, guilt-free consumption, think of potato chips as the next wave of health food. The crunch of fifteen chips supplies twice the potassium of a glass of orange juice and as much fiber as four slices of cracked wheat bread.

Potato Chips:

Practically every potato chip in the United States starts life as a spud in Michigan.

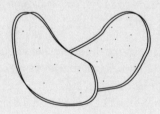

you know you're in
michigan when...
...Port Huron is pronounced "Port Urine"

Anyone in Michigan will flatly deny having an accent, insisting it's Michigan-speak that sets the standards for national broadcasters. Yet linguists and those without a hearing aid may argue with them.

Life keeps getting faster, and sometimes our cold lips can't keep up. Word endings such as "-ing" or "-ly" are often clipped, resulting in "Real good talkin' to ya." The letter *t* in the middle of "little" gets mushed into "liddle." And then there's the flat, nasally *a* leaving one to question if Ian is actually a girl named Ann.

Grand Rapids, the first city in the United States to put fluoride (or is that "flooride?") in its water has often been spoken as one word, "Granrapids." Port Huron is subject to interpretation as either "Port Yearn" or "Port Urine."

Ignore the spelling. Mackinac Island, in the Upper Peninsula, is pronounced the same as Mackinaw City, in the Lower Peninsula, and the same as the Straits of Mackinac, running through both peninsulas. Awww, that should be easy to remember.

Pronunciations:

Just as former U of M sportscaster Bob Ufer excitedly yelled "Meeeechigan," most residents have their own way of saying the name of their state.

Of course the name "Michigan" poses its own challenges. Derived from the Algonquian Chippewa Indian word *meicig-ama,* meaning "big sea water" or the Great Lakes, it's not unusual to hear someone proudly say they live in "Mitchigan."

you know you're in
michigan when...
...Hollywood comes home

Many celebrities get an adrenaline rush when they see the word *Hollywood* spelled out high in the hills. It's the same thrill that actor, playwright, director, singer, and all-around rare bird Jeff Daniels gets when he sees the sign welcoming him home: Chelsea, population 4,398.

Daniels credits Michigan for teaching him things he's never forgotten: how to play golf at age nine (eventually acquiring a seven handicap), and how to perpetuate movie-star status while living in a small town. After serving time as an English major at Central Michigan University, he made fruitful career-building stops in New York and California, but his beloved Midwestern roots kept reverberating, "Come back to me."

In 1991 Daniels opened the Purple Rose Theatre in an early 1900s car-and-bus garage formerly owned by his grandfather, thus bringing hundreds of thousands of playgoers to Chelsea, a city they may never have heard of before. Daniels remains committed to making it a showcase for Midwestern playwrights and actors. The intimate, 168-seat nationally acclaimed regional theater is as unpretentious as its founder.

Another of the *Terms of Endearment* and *Dumb and Dumber* star's goals was to

Purple Rose Theatre:

Chelsea's answer to the bright lights of Broadway, founded by one of the town's most popular citizens, actor Jeff Daniels.

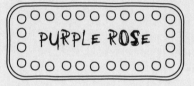

return home and make movies. His *Escanaba in Da Moonlight,* the story of five Yoopers on the eve of deer hunting opening day, was filmed entirely in the Upper Peninsula. Jackson, in the Lower Peninsula, was somewhat less fortunate as the stage for *Super Sucker,* the story of two door-to-door vacuum cleaner salesmen and their suspenseful competition that keeps you on the edge of your carpet. Nonetheless, through Daniels's hard work, they're two from the big screen that bear that all-important "Made in Michigan" label.

you know you're in
michigan when...
...your flannel underwear is showing

Sub-zero temperatures and a 1930s wardrobe malfunction together changed the course of history for Cedar Springs.

During the nation's bone-chilling winter of 1936, a New York reporter wrote in outrage that there was no flannel underwear to be found "anywhere." Not true, thought two enterprising Michigan women who had played peek-a-boo with red long johns hanging from men's trousers as they walked down the street. They fired back a response, "Just because Saks Fifth Avenue doesn't carry red flannels, doesn't mean that no one in the country does. Cedar Springs has red flannels."

The Associated Press printed their claim coast to coast, soon flooding the tiny town outside Grand Rapids with orders for flaming fanny warmers. A booming business began, eventually growing into the internationally famous Cedar Springs Red Flannel Factory. Their illustrious flap has been worn by Pres. Gerald Ford and converted into a blanket for Caroline Kennedy's pony, Macaroni.

Drop-seated underwear is Cedar Springs's official logo, with wooden cut-out versions hanging from lampposts most of the year. While some don't mind wearing their undies on their sleeve, the chief of the six-person police force is concerned that

respect for his authority might hit bottom when citizens eye his red flannel badge.

But red continues as mandatory attire for autumn's Red Flannel Festival, an annual excuse since 1939 to air your laundry in public.

Almost anything red flannel is available through the newly reorganized Cedar Springs Red Flannel Company, 37 North Main Street (616–696–9651). Festival information can be obtained at www.redflannel day.com.

Red Flannel Festival:

One weekend a year, Cedar Springs drops the red flannel seat that made it famous.

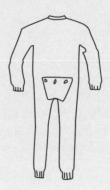

Sports professionals are often superstitious. For example, baseball players on a hitting streak are said to have their lucky "unwashed" socks. But leave it to Detroit Red Wings' fans to come up with a somewhat less couth "lucky" tradition—flinging an octopus across the ice during playoff games.

Owners of a Detroit fish market, Peter and Jerry Cusimano, were the co-creators of the now-famous custom when on April 15, 1952, they first tossed an eight-legged cephalopod against the boards of Olympia Stadium.

There was a method to their madness. In those days the National Hockey League had only six teams, meaning that eight wins—one for each tentacle—would get you the Stanley Cup. That year the Wings were the big winners, and their lucky charm has been with them ever since.

And apparently it works, giving the home team an extra leg up on the competition. The Detroit Red Wings have gone on to win more Stanley Cups than any other American hockey team. (Wouldn't you know da Canadians have won more, eh?)

Over the years the octopus phenomenon has grown to monumental proportions. During the 1995 playoffs two fans hurled a thirty-eight-pounder; the following year

Red Wings:

Detroit's beloved hockey team, helped along (some believe) by the toss of a dead octopus.

they pumped it up to a fifty-pound 'pus, which became the hood ornament for the Zamboni between periods.

Although People for the Ethical Treatment of Animals and team management have tried to squelch the mollusk-tossing practice, it continues in a somewhat more genteel fashion.

With each hockey-bound octopus purchase, Royal Oak's Superior Fish Market packages plastic gloves, hand wipes, and an Octoquette guide instructing the buyer to boil the octopus for thirty minutes pregame so that ice-cleaning crews have less slime on their hands.

you know you're in
michigan when...
...Hall of Famers rock

Michigan's own Bob Seger said it best:
Still like that old-time rock-and-roll
That kind of music just soothes my soul
In 2004 Seger and his indigenous blue-collar music—a far cry from his bass-ukulele playing days at age ten—joined some thirty other musicians from the state as members of the National Rock and Roll Hall of Fame; a cue to the world that Michigan Rocks.

Some of the other famers include Aretha "never travel by airplane" Franklin, whom we all "R-E-S-P-E-C-T" for continuing to reside here; Grand Rapids-born Del Shannon, whose 1961 hit "Runaway" sold 80,000 copies a day; Bill Haley and his twenty-two-million seller "Rock Around the Clock"; and Hank Ballard, composer of every chiropractor's favorite, "The Twist."

Not inducted into any hall that we know of: native Detroiter Larry LaPrise, whose classic "Hokey Pokey" did make it into many a dance hall and wedding playlist for decades.

Food for thought: Why is it that Michigan musicians seem to shroud themselves behind pseudonyms? Kid Rock is really Robert James Ritchie. Oak Park's Was (Not Was) is the duo of Don Fagenson and David Was. Oakland Township's Marshall Mathers (residing in ousted Kmart CEO Chuck Conaway's former digs) is better known as Slim Shady or Eminem. No matter what their name, Michiganians rock.

Rock and Roll Hall of Famers:

Martha and the Vandellas (named for the Detroit street Van Dyke and for Della Reese) are among those Michiganians represented in the National Rock and Roll Hall of Fame.

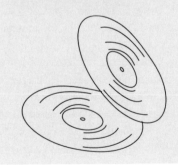

you know you're in
michigan when...
... you can play in a colossal sandbox

Traveling up the Lake Michigan shoreline you'll see so much sand, you might think you're in the Sahara. The truth is, you're in the midst of the world's largest accumulation of sand dunes around a body of fresh water.

Sand is as compatible with Michigan weather as a dog is with a fire hydrant. For the million years the sand has enjoyed residency here, it's been capitalizing on the strong lake breezes to create miles of monstrous bluffs, some towering more than 200 feet and still growing. Each year rare combinations of geologic forces expand and shift the dunes at a rate of almost 18 inches.

These dunes were made for walkin', talkin', campin', or in the case of the Silver Lake Sand Dunes State Park, slidin' down via motorized vehicle. Yes, this idyllic setting with its 450 acres of pristine sand is the only place east of Utah where you can actually drive on nature's sandbox. It's become an outdoor version of Disney's Space Mountain, with weekends packed with people zooming ninety miles per hour on their four-by-four trucks, dirt bikes, ATVs, and souped-up dune buggies.

Drive-yourself rentals are available at Sandy Korners, 1762 North Twenty-fourth Avenue in Mears (www.sandykorners.com). While the activity is not recommended for those with neck or back injuries, they do have a special "Pregnant Moms" tour. Everyone needs the experience of shaking sand out of their underwear at least once in their life.

Sand Dunes:

Within Lake Michigan's hundreds of acres of sandy shore stands Mt. Baldie, a 200-foot heap attracting vehicles to its peak in 1.9 seconds.

you know you're in
michigan when...

... the three little words you long to hear are *Sanders Hot Fudge*

For some it's more than a craving. It's a passion, a lust, provoking a state of ecstasy—and it comes out of a bottle. It's Sanders Hot Fudge, a milk chocolate fudge sauce like none other.

Fred Sanders, the creator of this euphoric delight, opened his retail candy business in downtown Detroit on June 17, 1875, when he kicked off a product line that grew to include perennial favorites such as chocolate honeycomb chips, chocolate bumpy cake, and, of course, his number-one dessert topping.

Today Sanders is owned by Clinton Township's Morley Candy Company, but the recipes all remain the same. What's the secret behind the hot fudge that drives people wild? The company says it's all in the cooking process. While countless competitors have tried to duplicate the recipe with ingredients of cream, liquid sugar, and chocolate, the temperature achieved while simmering in the topping "Jacuzzi" makes the difference, leaving a subtle hint of caramel.

One of Sanders's first online customers was a doctor from Japan, who acquired his obsession while in U of M Medical School in Ann Arbor. His hot fudge order came to $45. When told his shipping charges would be $100, he said he didn't care, and the 128-ounce cans were soon crossing the Pacific.

The sinfully rich topping has traveled to Australia, Germany, and the Middle East. Sanders's Diane Lynch says "the only place we haven't shipped to is the moon, but now that we're doing single-serving packets, who knows? That may just be next."

A dilemma for dieters, a single two-ounce serving contains 100 calories, 35 calories from fat.

Hot fudge fanciers can get their fix in the form of Sanders Hot Fudge Coffee (regular and decaf), Sanders Hot Fudge Ice Cream, or the original Sanders Hot Fudge Cream Puff.

Try a taste of Sanders at their candy and dessert shop in Laurel Park Place in Livonia; their headquarters on Hall Road, Clinton Township; or vicariously on www.sanders candy.com.

Sanders Hot Fudge:

The world's best, a thick, sinfully rich topping for ice cream, cream puffs, or anything that could use a little sweetening.

The job looks like it would be filled with joy and frivolity, save for the few screaming kids or occasional wet pants. How hard could it be to play Santa Claus? Hard enough for Michigan to lay claim to the world's oldest Santa Claus school.

Since 1937 the Charles W. Howard School has been teaching men and women (don't forget Mrs. Claus) how to share the love and laughter of the season. Tom Valent is the current dean, taking over the reins in 1987. No, he doesn't look like Santa. He doesn't have to. Just one listen to his "Ho, ho, ho" and you'll know he's the real thing.

Hair and make-up go a long way in transforming anyone into Santa. That's part of the forty-hour curriculum. After learning the history of St. Nicholas, Santa students attend classes in singing, storytelling, handling media interviews, Santa sign language (in order to communicate with deaf children), and how to carry the spirit of Christmas in their heart.

Tom and his wife, Holly (her real name), don't have ordinary house pets. They have two reindeer, Comet and Cupid—both females, since unlike males, their antlers last throughout the entire winter. You must become licensed in driving a reindeer sleigh before you can graduate.

Who comes to Michigan to learn to be Santa? People from all walks of life and all corners of the globe. In 1995 the Valents conducted the first World Santa Summit in Greenland, 400 miles from the North Pole, with representatives from Germany, Ireland, Denmark, and Spain.

So the next time you give your Christmas wish list to that jolly old man in his bright red suit, with the perfectly coiffed hair and beard, know there's a good chance he got his MSW (Masters of Santa Work) here in Michigan.

Santa School:

Where red-and-white uniforms are required—and clean-shaven faces strictly prohibited.

michigan when...

...the Soo gives overused words a permanent boot

Sault Ste. Marie is the oldest city in Michigan, as well as the third-oldest and most mispronounced in the nation. You can blame that on the French, since it was their missionaries who first ventured into the area in hot pursuit of fish and fur. By 1668 Jesuit explorer Fr. Jacques Marquette took the town under his wing, paying tribute to the Virgin Mary with the name Sault Ste. Marie, or simply "The Soo."

Although French scholars have battled it out over the exact meaning of *sault,* general consensus places the loose translation as "to jump," referring to the ideal spot to enter the St. Mary's River and avoid the perilous rapids cascading down more than 20 feet, from Lake Superior into the lower lakes. Loosely interpreted to mean "Rapids of St. Mary," the city is articulated, as only an attorney could, as "sue Saint Marie."

Words play a prominent role in the local lab of higher learning, Lake Superior State University. As a publicity stunt in 1977, the school put out the "List of Words Banished from the Queen's English for Mis-use, Overuse, or General Uselessness," now an annually anticipated New Year's Day occurrence.

Banned the first year was "new dimension," as in "he'll bring a new dimension to the job" (meaning "I have no idea why he was

---

Sault Ste. Marie:

This is the American version of the Canadian city with the same name, separated only by water and a college trying to banish overused words from our vocabulary.

---

hired"). Others getting the boot: "fresh frozen" (is the result "stale thawed?") in 1989; "been there, done that" in 1996; "get a life" in 1997; and "safe and effective" (shouldn't this be an automatic FDA requirement?) in 2005. You can submit your entry to the Word Banishment Office at (888) 800–LSSU or via www.lssu.edu/banished. "And I approve this message" (also exiled in 2005).

Known as Shipwreck Coast, a treacherous 80-mile stretch of Lake Superior off Whitefish Point is the final resting place for a large portion of the 6,000 vessels that have lost their struggle to cross the Great Lakes.

The *Edmund Fitzgerald,* a 730-foot freighter and the largest on the "inland seas" for thirteen years, is among the most mysterious and controversial losses. Not a single distress call came in on the stormy night of November 10, 1975, when the ship, its captain and twenty-eight crew members disappeared 17 miles from shore. Nor, for the first time anyone could remember, was the lighthouse lit.

Thirteen sunken ships and their treasures are memorialized in the Great Lakes Shipwreck Museum, including the 200-pound bronze bell retrieved from the *Fitzgerald*'s wreckage on July 4, 1995—that night inexplicably becoming only the second time the lighthouse has ever been dark.

Shipwrecks throughout the Great Lakes have all been well-preserved by the frigid waters, guaranteeing divers "recreational exploration." State law governs the sport of diving, clearly differentiating the preserves from state parks, advising all underwater fortune-seekers to "Take nothing but pictures, leave nothing but bubbles."

To experience firsthand the eeriness of the night winds, book a room in the Shipwreck Museum's renovated 1923 crew members' quarters. Reservations can be made by calling (877) SHIPWRECK or going online at www.shipwreckmuseum.com. See if they leave the lighthouse on for you.

Shipwrecks:

The *Edmund Fitzgerald* with its cargo of 26,116 tons of taconite pellets is one of thousands of ships lying at the bottom of the Great Lakes.

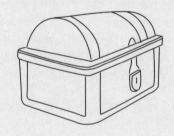

you know you're in
michigan when...
...42 million people follow your pattern

Fashion models epitomize a level of thinness difficult to match, even if one passes on that fourth piece of pizza. Yet, there's a single spot in the city of Niles where all the models are paper-thin, literally.

Inside the 740,000-square-foot manufacturing home of Simplicity Patterns, machines howl and hiss, as they have since 1931, spitting out the designer tissue-paper forms for millions of do-if-yourself sewers worldwide.

Ever wonder what becomes of old popsicle sticks or coffee filters? They could be in the pattern for your wedding dress. Almost everything's recyclable in their secret recipe paper-making process. When one major corporation changed banks, necessitating new checks, cases of their shredded blank checks became coat patterns.

Even cloth can be recycled. Muhammad Ali lives down the road from the plant in Berrien Springs, and his daughter is a member of Simplicity's New York design team. With a little coaxing, perhaps she'll create a pattern of one of the Champ's famous robes so faraway places like Australia, Mexico, or South Africa can stitch their own version of a Michigan original.

Over time, automation has forced some changes to their printing, distribution, and handling. Take for instance, the one thousand people whose job each day was to meticulously fold each pattern and stuff it into the envelope without a tear. Three machines now do that.

Simplicity gives group tours for twelve or more with a two-week advance notice (reserve by calling 269–683–4100, ext. 565). Be sure to wear closed-toe shoes for the two-hour behind-the-scenes outing.

Simplicity Patterns:

All of the company's more-than-1,600 patterns for home-sewn clothes, costumes, and home furnishings are made in Niles, Michigan.

you know you're in
michigan when...
...guns fire snow

"They're bare out there.... Load up the guns!" A hunter's charge? Kinda. In Michigan, the words signal a hot pursuit ... for snow. That may be hard to believe coming from a state where annual snowfalls, in some spots, can go as high as 30 feet.

Why look for more? Because downhill snow skiing and snowboarding is a $146-million industry here. When there's not enough white stuff, you're out of business.

Resort owners on both peninsulas are the first to say, "When you don't like the weather in Michigan, do something about it." So when the hills start looking worn, out come the snow-making machines to begin an Extreme Makeover, Michigan-style.

No phony fillers here. Using water and high pressure, the plumping-up material released is the real thing—100 percent manmade snow, more dense and durable than nature's creation. Roughly 10 inches of natural snow adds just 1 inch to the snow's base. But 10 inches of machine-made fluff and you've got 7 more inches on top. The magic begins at 28; degrees that is. The colder it gets, the more snow you can make.

Competition is stiff, so much so that ski resorts manufacture and patent their own ski guns. Nub's Nob in Harbor Springs runs 224 of their secret snow guns to fire up their forty-nine ski runs.

Even western U.P., boasting the longest ski season in the country, needs a lift from technology to open the slopes at least a week before Thanksgiving and keep them hopping along through April, causing the Easter Bunny to be concerned about freezing his tail off.

Snow Guns:

Cannon-like snow-making devices, guaranteeing that all forty-four of the state's ski resorts will have a white Christmas ... and Easter.

you know you're in
michigan when...
...good grooming means a trail of combed snow

Kids in Michigan grow up with an appreciation for the family winter sport of sledding, whether it's going downhill on a highfalutin' toboggan or on an inverted trash can lid. Most agree the best part of growing up is getting a faster sled.

Come winter, the Motor Capital of the world doesn't relinquish its title just because there's a few yards of snow on the ground. After all, the very first snowmobile, an overgrown sleigh with an airplane propeller on the back, was powered by a Ford Model T engine. Anything you can do in a car, you can do colder and faster in a snowmobile.

At last count, Michigan had 431,630 registered snowmobiles, more than any other state. Many of them are owned by serious sledders who squeeze themselves into insulated snowsuits, looking as if they're ready to land on the moon instead of heading for the more-than-6,500 miles of groomed trails the state offers.

Some may complain about the noise level of the snow machines—that is until they hear the sound of their one billion dollars *cha-chinging* into the economy. Some poor soul even gave up his time on the trails to determine that the average Michigan snowmobiler spends $4,218 each year on vacations and equipment.

Snowmobiling:

Michigan leads the nation in the number of registered snowmobiles.

Owners of snowmobile dealerships may be the happiest of all to see the snow season melt away, since the end of April is reportedly their peak selling period, after the banks have cashed all the sledders' tax refund checks.

For information on trails, rentals, or anything else to do with moving on snow, contact the Michigan Snowmobile Association at (616) 361–2285, (800) 246–0206, or www.msasnow.org.

you know you're in
michigan when...
...the thermometer reads 98.6 inches

It's a tough job, but somebody's got to do it: stand in the ground year-round stylishly pointing, a la Vanna White, to the current snow depth as passersby all *ooh* and *ahh*. In Michigan they're known as snow thermometers, usually large painted sticks with movable crossbars.

Mancelona's had one for two decades. Standing about 25 feet tall at the corner of 131st and State Streets, the orange-and-black gauge is dedicated to the high school's Ironmen mascot.

The U.P. calls for heavy-duty, Paul Bunyan-sized thermometers. None is more popular than the 32-footer on U.S. Highway 41 at the top of Cliff Hill, north of Mohawk. This big gauge has been a big hit with tourists since it was first erected in the 1950s. Originally a pulley would raise the bar on a daily basis. But even the pulley soon grew tired of the cold, often freezing in mid-action. After a couple of years, a replacement bar was installed, with the much easier task of moving only once at the end of snow season (occasionally as late as May).

A plaque alongside cites the winter of 1978–79 as the biggest snowfall: 390.4 inches, an east-of-the-Rockies record. The all-time low was 81.3 inches, set in

Snow Thermometers:

Towering measuring sticks stuck in the earth to measure the amounts of annual snowfall.

1930–31. The year 2005 brought about a complete renovation of the Cliff Hill thermometer, with new paint—still a white base and a red marker—and new wooden panels.

Snow is a time-honored tradition in these parts. Greg Patrick of the Keweenaw Road Commission, the thermometer's keeper, admits that "If we weren't up to our eyeballs in snow, we wouldn't have a job." And neither would the guy who developed the desktop replica of Michigan's snow thermometer, a hot seller.

you know you're in
michigan when...
...ships ride their own elevator

Traffic can be a headache in Michigan, both on the roads and on the water. Since 1855 the Soo Locks in Sault Ste. Marie have been helping ease the pain of vessels traveling to the Great Lakes via the St. Mary's River. With 5,000 ships passing through each year, the Locks are one of the biggest and busiest traffic waterways in the world.

The locks allow both "lakers" and "salties" (ocean-faring ships) to safely drop or be lifted to compensate for the 21-foot difference between the river and Lakes Michigan, Superior, and Huron. This task is initiated, literally, by the click of a button,

The two locks in use today are sized to handle the biggest of the big—those vessels carrying more than 72,000 tons of cargo, usually iron ore, coal, cement, or grain.

Traveling through the Locks (currently owned by the U.S. government and operated by the U.S. Army Corps of Engineers) could be the deal of the century. It's free for everyone. When is the last time you heard of the government giving away anything for free?

From the upper level of the visitor center, you can watch the excitement of the freighters being "locked" through. Or you can be "locked" in yourself on one of several operating tour ships.

Trip planning tip number one: The locks are closed between January 15 and March 25—sometimes longer depending on the weather.

Trip planning tip number two: Bring your tallest boots in December, and maybe a flag if you're less than five feet tall. On December 12, 1995, a five-day storm in Sault Ste. Marie culminated by dumping 61.7 inches of snow.

Soo Locks:

Dinner cruises on the world-famous locks can either lift your spirits or give your stomach that sinking feeling.

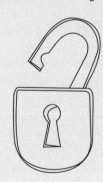

The word *tailgate* takes on new meaning in Michigan during autumn weekends. Ordinarily one thinks of "tailgating" as driving too close to the car in front of you, resulting in a hefty fine, some points against your driving record, or possibly just a single-finger salute.

Come football season, "tailgating" becomes one big supercharged picnic, usually centered out of the rear end of an SUV. The quirky ritual has become so popular that every football weekend, an estimated half-million Michiganders fill their coolers with beverages and artery-clogging foods, pack up half their living rooms, and head out to one of the state's high school, collegiate, or pro games.

Both vehicle and driver are decked out in the appropriate school colors, ready to tackle the task of finding a precious parking spot. In Ann Arbor (a.k.a. A2), that means heading to the University of Michigan golf course, where cars park everywhere except the greens. An alternative might be a nearby house, where big bucks will get you a spot anywhere on the owner's green lawn. In East Lansing, at MSU, the tennis courts provide plum parking.

Then the real fun begins, rolling out the tables and the tents, the gadgets and the grills, the beer and the brats. (Against

Tailgate Parties:

A pre-game excuse to celebrate your school's football prowess before the team loses.

Memphis State, brats may be replaced with peanut-butter-and-banana sandwiches, if you're into "theme" parties.)

Next the group stands beside their vehicle for hours laughing, eating, drinking, and looking for a place to go to the bathroom before those who are ticketless settle in comfortably to watch the game off satellite dish on a big-screen TV.

you know you're in
michigan when...
...lakes are lovely

If you think of Michigan's inland lakes as precious gems, Antrim County's Torch Lake is the Hope Diamond. Local buzz is that *National Geographic* listed it as the third most beautiful lake in the world, though no one can remember when and no one cares anyway, because it should have placed first.

Surrounded by a shoreline of lush towering greens, its trademark sparkling turquoise blue water is a leftover of the ancient glaciers, although it appears as if it was airlifted yesterday from the Caribbean.

In sharp contrast to the proportions of the state's population, Torch Lake is tall—18 miles long—and skinny—2½ miles at its widest—and the bearer of a sand-exfoliated smooth bottom. In most places it's also deep, 111 feet on average, 330 feet at its max. Except for the south end's 100-acre sand bar where you'll find hundreds of boats anchored as party animals, dogs included, thrash around in 3 feet of crystal clear water.

This northern tropic has become a haven for the rich (nothing's cheap here) and famous. Controversial movie director Michael Moore is a year-round resident, while the voice of blue-haired Marge Simpson, Julie Kavner, and actress Christine Lahti are summer-time "Torchies."

On Torch Lake, the hub for the cruise-worthy Chain of Lakes, it's BYOB (bring your own boat), or you can rent from one of the many marinas. Either way, be sure to make a landing at The Dockside, at 6340 Old Torch Lake Drive in Bellaire (231–377–7777). This popular outdoor watering hole (sunburned boaters can stay inside) provides a taste of folksy camaraderie along with its signature Torch Lake lemonade and useful lake lore.

Torch Lake:

In Michigan, you're never more than 6 miles from an inland lake. Torch is said to be among the prettiest in the world.

you know you're in
michigan when...
...almost everyone has their own town, even Ralph

Lansing, Michigan: named after John Lansing, Revolutionary War Hero; Saginaw, Michigan: named after the Indian Tribe Ralph, Michigan: named after Ralphs everywhere whose name has caused them to suffer through a lifetime of abuse.

It's quite an honor to have a city named after you, and Michigan gets an A+ at paying tribute to folks who probably never thought, or may not have realized, that somewhere within the state, there is a town or city named just for them.

Here's a list of names that should improve the self-esteem of the chosen few:

Adrian	Constantine	Lamont
Allen	Crystal	Leonard
Arnold	Curtis	LeRoy
Arthur	Douglas	Leslie
Ashley	Elmer	Lucas
Ashton	Elsie	Luther
Austin	Emmett	Marcellus
Beebe	Freda	Marne
Beulah	Frederic	Martin
Bradley	Glenn	Melvin
Brutus	Gregory	Nathan
Burt	Harvey	Paris
Byron	Holly	Pearl
Carleton	Homer	Ralph
Clare	Hope	Ray
Clifford	Ida	Romeo
Clinton	Isabella	Ruby
Clyde	Lacy	Ruth

Selma	Taylor	Wallace
Sharon	Theodore	Whitney
Sherman	Vernon	Willard
Sylvester	Victoria	Willis

Please forgive me if there is a Michigan city named after you I missed. Only single, first names were considered, forcing the exemption of Bruce Crossing (since I couldn't find a listing for anyone with the first name of Bruce and a surname of Crossing).

Extensive research on the city of Ralph, sitting almost smack dab in the middle of the U.P., found four roads—one paved and three gravel—a population of fifty-one, and a post office (open mornings only), with a sticker on the front door reading, "I love Ralph, Michigan."

Towns with Names for Names:

An example of the changing name game, Michigan pays equal tribute to the common man and woman as well as the more extraordinary one.

you know you're in
michigan when...
...tulips are more popular than rock stars

Holland, Michigan, is a town of 35,000 residents and six million tulips.

Everywhere you turn in this conservative section of western Michigan, you'll feel the influence of the Dutch settlers of 1847. Just open the local phone book and you'll find pages of surnames beginning with "Van," making it convenient for trading monogrammed hand-me-downs.

But the heart of the area comes to life in May, when millions of sleepy tulip bulbs burst out of the earth in a rainbow of colors. Every year since 1929, floral fascination consumes an eight-day festival affectionately known as Tulip Time, attracting such national attention that *Reader's Digest* once declared it the Number One Small Town Festival in America.

Tourists come from near and far to check out the blossoms devouring the city. There's millions of 'em in the 6-mile stretch of Tulip Lane. On Windmill Island: another 175,000. The Depot on Lincoln Avenue: 22,000. Window on the Waterfront: 100,000. Everywhere your eye takes you, there are tulips. And each year more get sowed, since the life expectancy of a single plant is only two to three years.

You can look, but you cannot touch. Tulips are taken so seriously here that there's a

> **Tulip Time:**
>
> When the residents of western Michigan take cleanliness to new heights, pounding the pavement with buckets and brooms to prepare for the tulip festival.

$100 fine if you're caught harvesting one, and yes, pickers have paid the penalty.

When the last bloom has fallen at Veldheer's Tulip Gardens, the guard changes and more than a million day lilies take over for the rest of the summer.

For Tulip Festival information visit www.tuliptime.com or (800) 822–2770. Veldheer's at 12755 Quincy Street stays open through bulb-planting season each fall. Call (616) 399–1900 or visit www .veldheertulipgardens.com.

93

...football rivalries are bigger than presidential elections

Major decisions are made in autumn. It's a toss-up in Michigan as to which outcome has more importance: (a) Who will be the next president; or (b) who will be the next Big Ten football champion.

If you answered (b), chances are you have some fondness for the University of Michigan, whose football team has been on the winning side of the Big Ten for decades.

Next question: Which gridiron rivalry is met with more heart-stopping anticipation: (a) U of M versus MSU; or (b) U of M versus OSU?

If you answered (a) you're a Spartan; (b) you're a Wolverine.

Wolverines favor the Ohio State competition because it's been going on longer, the premier battle having taken place in 1903. The competition with Michigan State didn't start until 1953, when the former Michigan State College entered the Big Ten.

Often the Big Ten championship is decided with the Ohio State game, which some refer to as the biggest rivalry in the nation. Recent history saw it as a showdown between the late Woody Hayes and his former player and assistant coach, Bo Schembechler. After twenty years, the latter retired from U of M in 1989 as the winningest active coach in the nation, having never lost a season, yet never winning a national championship either.

U of M Versus MSU:

This long-standing, less-than-friendly rivalry even has a chain of stores devoted to it, The Great Divide.

The Michigan State matchup (often called the Great Divide, forcing some families to become a version of the Hatfields and the McCoys), competes for another biggie—the Paul Bunyan trophy. Almost a big ten itself, the Michigan pine carving stands at least 8 feet tall, wearing a cap, shirt, and blue-green pants. He's been described by U of M coach Lloyd Carr as "the ugliest trophy in college football." How ugly is it? So ugly the Wolverines said they would refuse it if they won the first year it was awarded. Not to worry, they lost, 14–6.

The victories have changed hands several times over the years. At the end of the 2004 season, Michigan's record against Ohio State was 57–38–6; and against MSU it was 64–28–5.

The Spartans don't fret over it too much. They say wait until basketball season.

...you take Vernors instead of Tums

The number-one "must have" in any gift basket from Michigan is Vernors Ginger Ale. The Detroit-born, funky, carbonated beverage has been a remedy for people's problems for decades. Bad tummy? Take Vernors. Bad hair day? Take Vernors. Bad marriage? Take Vernors. You get the picture for this better-than-Prozac, feel-good liquid.

Indirectly, the Civil War was responsible for its creation. Pharmacist James Vernor placed a secret mixture of nineteen ingredients, including ginger, vanilla, and natural flavorings, in an oak barrel, just before he was called to duty. When he returned four years later, he found his concoction had been transformed by the aging process into a drink with an indescribable gingery taste, which he simply called "Vernors," a term that in Michigan is as generic to ginger ale as Kleenex is to tissue.

His first soda fountain opened in 1896, with the product's popularity mushrooming the fountain into a full-fledged bottling plant where you could sip the product for one small nickel.

Tours of the operations were the highlight of many Boy and Girl Scout field trips. There's likely not a local baby boomer who doesn't remember their first sample of Vernors and the zesty tickle the magical fizz created as it went up their nose.

The company has been through many changes since the Vernor family first sold it to an investment group in 1966. Now owned by Cadbury Schweppes Americas Beverages, the ginger ale's availability has been limited to a dozen states, mostly in the Midwest, with scattered offerings in California and Florida to accommodate displaced Michiganders.

But the saddest change may have been the elimination of the Vernor's gnome from the label. The happy-go-lucky fellow has been replaced by another typically boring logo.

One more thing: The city of Boston owes us big time. The official ingredients for a Boston Cooler are vanilla ice cream and Vernors ginger ale.

Vernors Ginger Ale:

A unique, bubbly ginger ale that for decades has been consumed to cure anything that ails you.

you know you're in
michigan when...
...the fireplace is still burning on the Fourth of July

Humorists have a field day with Michigan's weather, which is often as unpredictable as Madonna's hair color.

Like most places, it gets cold in the winter. It got as low as 51 degrees below zero a couple of times: on February 9, 1934, in Vanderbilt, and February 4, 1996, in Amasa.

And the summers can get pretty hot. Michigan's steamiest day was 112 degrees on July 13, 1936, in Mio.

But is there really any merit to a claim such as "If you don't like the weather in Michigan, wait ten minutes and it'll change"?

Let's attempt to sort out fact from fiction.

It's been said: "You Know You're in Michigan When . . .

. . . the sky drops hail the size of a hockey puck."

Fact: On March 27, 1991, in Portage, storms produced hailstones 4.5 inches in diameter.

The diameter of an official NFL hockey puck is only 3 inches.

" . . . you can wear a swimsuit and a snow-suit on the same day."

Fact: In Detroit at 1:00 P.M on March 8, 1987, the temperature was 74 degrees. By 1:00 P.M. on March 9, the thermometer had plummeted to 23 degrees, registering the largest change ever: a 51-degree drop in 24 hours.

" . . . both corn and snow banks are knee-high by the Fourth of July."

Fact: On August 8, 1882, a Lake Michigan snowstorm dumped 6 inches on a ship's deck. More recently, Sault Ste. Marie saw a snow/ice/rain mixture on August 27, 1986. There's never been any accumulation in July.

" . . . the last snow of the season cancels the May Day Dance."

Fact: Marquette was blanketed by 22.4 inches of snow on May 10, 1990.

Finally, just for the record: The snowiest winter in Michigan was 1978–79, with a whopping 391.9 inches; and it actually occurred in Delaware . . . MI.

Weather:

Like the nursery rhyme, when it's hot in Michigan, it's very, very hot; when it's cold, it's very, very cold; and, every now and then, it's just right.

you know you're in
michigan when...
...white pines rise

The white pine is Michigan's official state tree. The ones in Grayling's Hartwick Pines State Park are in an enviable position. At more than 350 years old, they've shown no signs of elderly shrinkage, standing with their spines soldier straight at a stellar 160 feet with a firm 6-foot girth.

This somewhat miraculous 49-acre patch of pine, affectionately dubbed Old Growth, is the largest survivor of Michigan's logging era. From 1840 to 1910 lumberjacks were going gangbusters. More trees here lost their trunks to the teeth of a saw blade than anywhere else in the country. But unexplainably these white pines were spared.

Arborists have a field day in this forest. So many came to gawk at what was the state's largest tree—a gangling 190-foot monarch pine—that a barricading fence became necessary. With no shield from the wind, the monster pine lost 30 feet in a 1996 storm, ultimately causing its demise. Curiosity seekers still clamor for a look, frequently inquiring at the visitor center as to the whereabouts of "the big dead tree." You can go ask yourself—the entrance to Hartwick Pines State Park, the Lower Peninsula's largest state park, is at 4216 Ranger Road, Grayling, or call (989) 348–7068.

About 75 miles to the southwest is one man's lifetime tribute to the pine. This is where, in the 1930s, William Overholzer built a cabin and all of its 200 pieces of furniture entirely out of naturally fallen pine. Shrine of the Pines is still intact, with a dining table carved from a 700-pound stump and a rocking chair so perfectly balanced it swings precisely fifty-five times with a single push. With the world's largest collection of rustic pine furniture, the home is open mid-May through mid-October, on Highway 37, 2 miles south of Baldwin. Call (616) 745–7892 for more information.

White Pine:

A virgin forest and a family's home exemplify the multi-tasking ability of the state's official tree.

...a non-resident weasels its way into becoming the state's mascot

Although "The Wolverine State" has been one of Michigan's nicknames since the 1830s, no one knows why for certain. Wolverines aren't indigenous to the state. In fact no one can remember the last time they saw one outside of a zoo. Until February 2004 that is, when a single male was sighted roaming through Ubley in Huron County (near the top of Michigan's thumb).

Described as bulky and bear-like, the wolverine resembles a badger but is technically a member of the weasel family. Carnivorous wolverines, though nasty and gluttonous, are neither hunters nor fighters (smaller prey excluded), and generally feed off any and all leftovers from other wildlife.

Perhaps that's the reason Ohio is thought to be responsible for our Wolverine nickname. During a dispute over Toledo around 1835, Ohioans described Michiganians to be as bloodthirsty for land as this animal is for food. (Toledo went to Ohio, ultimately making us victorious.)

Native Americans may also have contributed to our moniker. When expressing their displeasure in the loss of their land, they compared greedy settlers to wolverines.

In the 1920s the University of Michigan adopted the wolverine as its official mas-

Wolverines:

The meanest member of the weasel family, the state mascot once was affiliated with two universities at the same time.

cot, and at the request of then-coach Fielding Yost, two caged wolverines were carried in by the players before each football game. Quickly growing in size and voracity, the pair was soon retired to a local zoo.

What most people don't realize is that Michigan State had the nickname long before their arch-rival U of M. From 1900 to 1974, MSU's yearbook was called *The Wolverine,* but in 1975 they relinquished the title. Today, aptly named for the river running through campus, the Spartan's annual is known as *Red Cedar Log.*

you know you're in
michigan when...
... wooden shoes are part of the daily uniform

When the Holland High School Marching Band begins to play, everyone listens—and looks on—in awe. For as they blast out "Tiptoe through the Tulips," band members create intricate formations and do some high stepping dance routines, and all the while their feet are in unforgiving wooden shoes. Yes, Dutch dancers in full costume carry the flag of the Netherlands, and the drum majors kick as high as they can, all while wearing their lumber loafers. Walking in those things is tough enough; marching in them should earn one a podiatrist's gold medal.

The secret behind the sole is how you sock it. Members stuff up to six pairs of socks in their shoes to avoid having to take Band-Aid breaks. Over the years those socks have cushioned marchers' feet for many miles in the Presidential Inaugural Parade, Tournament of Roses Parade, Disney World Main Street Parade, and of course, Holland's annual Tulip Time Parade.

It helps that an abundance of master wooden shoemakers are in the neighborhood. Nearby Dutch Village has some of everything Old Holland has to offer, whether it's the traditional blue delftware, or for the person who has everything, a pair of customized wooden golf shoes. Talk about playing with a handicap.

Dutch Village's Wooden Shoe Shop advises giving them a cut-out pattern of your feet, but phone orders can also be placed at (800) 285–7177. Information on their theme park and other shops is available at (616) 396–1475 or www.dutchvillage.com.

Wooden Shoes:

Brides can clomp down the aisle in a custom-made pair of Holland's wooden wedding shoes.

you know you're in
michigan when...
... youse meet da yooper

Generally thought of as backwoods folk, let it be known that yoopers do have indoor plumbing and their own language, or at least their own dialect.

Yoopanese has its roots based in the melting pot of ethnicities that have settled in the U.P., mainly American Indian, Italian, French Canadian, Swedish, Finnish, and Croatian.

Let's start with a couple simple grammar lessons: "You" refers to just one person; the plural, as in "you all" or "you guys," is "youse." Since the Finns don't use prepositions or articles, neither do most yoopers, announcing, "I'm going post office" or "Youse go mall." And then there's the Canadian influence of ending a sentence with "eh." Youse got all dat, eh? (*Th*'s are tough for dem yooper speak.)

Vocabulary is a bit easier. Hunting cabins are "camps." "Lakers" are lake trout. "Pank," an old mining term, is "to pack." Thus where you'd originally pank powder into a blasting hole, now "youse pank down your laundry fit more before you go camp catch lakers."

Yoopers are the first to poke fun at themselves. Da Yooper Tourist Trap in Ishpeming is an overloaded gift shop featuring Big

Ernie, "Da world's largest working shotgun", "a yooper briefcase" consisting of a pair of jockey shorts with handles; and all the punk-to-polka CDs ever pressed by the satirical musical quintet, "Da Yoopers."

When state representatives once considered making Yoopanese the official state dialect, Da Yoopers voiced their own Declaration of Independence in a song to the governor:

> You better turn us loose
> We asked you for some rest stops
> Instead you gave us moose.
> The honeymoon is over
> The declaration's written
> We'll take what's above the bridge
> And you can keep the mitten.

Yoopers:

A slang term referring to anyone residing in the Upper Peninsula, or U.P. (pronounced "you pee").

you know you're in
michigan when...
...you cross the Zilwaukee Bridge

Zilwaukee, Michigan. Just where is this funny sounding town? Pick up your right hand, as if you're making a Michigan map, and find the center of the *u* between your thumb and base of your index finger. Go down about a quarter of an inch. Voila! You're in Zilwaukee.

For years, when people knew they were heading this way, they'd pack up their car with enough provisions to last a week. What is it about this town of only 1,799 people (as of the 2000 census) that has dramatically affected so many lives in the state? The answer could be the basis for a movie: "The Bridges of Saginaw County."

The first bridge was a four-lane drawbridge to get traffic over the Saginaw River. Opening in 1960, it soon caused more trouble than it eliminated. When the bridge went up, traffic backed up and tempers flared up; so much so that one frustrated deer hunter reportedly got out of his truck, took his rifle, and shot a round through the unpopular bridge controller's booth.

The Michigan Department of Transportation took the hint. A new bridge was going to be built.

In typically prompt government action, building of the replacement structure commenced almost twenty years later, in 1979, with a budget of $77 million. There were

Zilwaukee Bridge:

The building of the Zilwaukee Bridge reads like the Neverending Story.

rough seas this time, too. Four years into the project a major construction accident brought work to a halt while the driving headaches continued.

It was a Christmas present for motorists when the northbound lanes of I–75 finally opened on December 23, 1987. Travel on the southbound lanes followed almost nine months later. All this and a grand total of $124.3 million in expenses.

United happily ever after, the "Z" Bridge sees 90,000 to 100,000 vehicles daily.

But perhaps the two faces with the biggest smiles belong to Dan and Samuel Johnson, who founded Z-town in 1848. The brothers wanted to attract more workers to their saw mill, so they labeled their new town Zilwaukee, purposely hoping it would be confused with Milwaukee.

index

THE INSIDER'S SOURCE

With more than 120 Midwest-related titles, we have the area covered. Whether you're looking for the path less traveled, a favorite place to eat, family-friendly fun, a breathtaking hike, or enchanting local attractions, our pages are filled with ideas to get you from one state to the next.

For a complete listing of all our titles, please visit our Web site at www.GlobePequot.com. The Globe Pequot Press is the largest publisher of local travel books in the United States and is a leading source for outdoor recreation guides.

FOR BOOKS TO THE MIDWEST

INSIDERS' GUIDE®

FALCON GUIDE®

Available wherever books are sold.
Orders can also be placed on the Web at www.GlobePequot.com, by phone from 8:00 A.M. to 5:00 P.M. at 1-800-243-0495, or by fax at 1-800-820-2329.